Welcome to
Microsoft®
Office 2016

JILL MURPHY
Custom Performance Solutions

LABYRINTH
LEARNING™

Berkeley, CA

President:
Brian Favro

Product Manager:
Jason Favro

Development Manager:
Laura Popelka

Production Manager:
Debra Grose

Senior Editor:
Alexandra Mummery

Junior Editor:
Alexandria Henderson

Composition:
Happenstance Type-o-rama

Cover Design:
Mick Koller, SuperLab Design

LABYRINTH
LEARNING™

Welcome to Microsoft Office 2016
by Jill Murphy

Labyrinth Learning
2560 9th Street, Suite 320
Berkeley, CA 94710
800.522.9746
On the web at lablearning.com

ITEM: 1-59136-970-3
ISBN-13: 978-159136-970-7

Manufactured in the United States of America

10 9 8 7 6 5 4 3 2 1

Table of Contents

CHAPTER 1: WORD
Working with Word Basics 1

CHAPTER 2: WORD
Writing a Letter and a Résumé 23

CHAPTER 3: WORD
Editing the Business Etiquette Column . . . 53

Preface

Welcome to Microsoft® Office 2016 provides a survey of the most popular Office 2016 applications: Word, Excel, PowerPoint, and Access. We begin with four Word chapters, which cover topics such as the Ribbon, navigation techniques, AutoComplete, tables, editing text, AutoCorrect, character formatting, special text effects, and more. In the two Excel chapters, learners enter and edit data, construct simple formulas, and depict data using column and pie charts. PowerPoint topics include creating a new presentation, working with layouts and design themes, creating animations and transitions, and more. Finally, in the Access chapter, learners create a new database and print datasheets.

Our Approach

For the last two decades, Labyrinth Learning has been working to perfect our *unique instructional design*. The benefit of our approach is that learning is faster and easier for everyone. Instructors have found that our approach works well in self-paced, instructor-led, and blended learning environments. The Labyrinth approach has many key features, including the following:

- *Concise concept discussions* are immediately followed by exercises that give students experience with those concepts right away.
- *Carefully selected figures* are placed in close proximity to the text, so no figure numbers are necessary.
- *Quick Reference sections* summarize key tasks with generic steps that will work without repeating an exercise. These tables are particularly useful during open-book tests and after the course is complete.
- *Hands-On exercises* are carefully written and repeatedly tested so they are absolutely reliable. Many exercise steps are illustrated with figures to make them easier to follow.
- *Skill Builder exercises* provide additional practice on key skills using less detailed instruction compared to Hands-On exercises.

Comprehensive Support

This course is supported with comprehensive instructor support materials that include printable solution guides for side-by-side comparisons, test banks, customizable assessments, customizable PowerPoint presentations, detailed lesson plans, preformatted files for integration with leading learning management systems, and more. Our unique WebSims allow students to perform realistic exercises for tasks that cannot be performed in the computer lab.

Visual Conventions

This book uses visual conventions and typographic cues to guide learners through the chapters. Some of the cues are indicated here.

CUE	WHAT IT DOES
Tip! **Note!** **Warning!**	Tips, notes, and warnings are used throughout the text to draw attention to certain topics.
QUICK REFERENCE:	Quick Reference tables provide generic instructions for key tasks. Only perform these tasks if you are instructed to do so in an exercise.
`Type this text`	Text to type using the keyboard is shown in this typeface.
Action words	Important action words in exercise steps are shown in bold.
Command→ **Command→Command**	Multistep Ribbon commands are presented like this. For example, **Home→Font→Bold** means to go to the Home tab, go to the Font command group, and click the Bold button.
HANDS-ON	Hands-On exercises appear immediately after concept discussions. They provide detailed, step-by-step tutorials that help you master the skills presented.
	Self-Assessment sections include true/false and multiple choice questions designed to gauge your understanding of the concepts and skills introduced in the chapter.
	Skill Builder exercises test your new skills by describing the desired, correct results without providing all the detail on how to achieve them.

Quick Reference Table Summary

Word Tasks

Excel Tasks

PowerPoint Tasks

Acknowledgements

Many individuals contribute to the development and completion of a textbook. We are grateful to the instructors and professionals who provided feedback and suggested improvements. This book has benefited from the feedback and suggestions of the following reviewers:

Debra Blencowe, *Collin College*

Sara Bozzuto, *Middlesex Community College*

Gert Brailsford, *Global Business Institute*

Menka Brown, *Piedmont Technical College*

Brenda Gayle Bryant, *The Gayle Group*

John Bullock, *Kirkwood Community College*

Marie Calarco, *Cuyahoga Valley Career Center*

Beverly Campbell, *TCCD*

Sherryl Carter, *Inglewood Unified School District/ Inglewood Community Adult School*

Robert Cook, *Martinez Adult Education*

Barbara R. Corzonkoff, *SMCOE/ROP and Skyline College*

Teresa Ferguson, *Seattle Vocational Institute*

Jason Holcomb, *Vatterott Educational Centers*

Gaylene Jones, *Summit College*

Kimberly Jones, *Bonds Career Center*

Dawn Kaiser, *Kirtland Community College*

Kevin Keehan, *Southwestern College*

Vicky Kelder, *Westchester Community College*

Peggy Kozy, *University of Phoenix*

Joanne Lauzon, *North Shore Community College*

Elaine Loughrey, *MiraCosta College*

Samantha Marchant, *North GA Tech*

Nikkea Masters, *Placer School for Adults*

Tom McGinn, *YCCC*

Julie Meyer, *McKendree University*

Jerry Mitchell, *Institute of Business & Medical Careers*

Chidmma Nwankwere, *Hi-Tech Charities*

Chesty Peterson, *Downy Adult School*

Richard Peterson, *South Seattle Community College*

George Riley, *Pickaway-Ross JVS*

Joseph Roy, *Madison Area Technical College*

Joyce Schlose, *Goodwill Industries of Denver*

Doris Scott, *Traviss Career Center*

Greg Simos, *Jefferson College*

Lisa Smith, *Moore Norman Technology Center*

Mary Spata, *Wilco Career Center*

Judy Spencer, *Central Oklahoma Juvenile Center*

Michelle Story, *Illinois Valley Community College*

Working with Word Basics

Microsoft Word is a powerful word-processing program, and no matter what your job or undertaking, you will likely need to create documents. In this chapter, you will learn Word basics, become familiar with the document interface, and use both the mouse and keyboard to navigate in a document.

LEARNING OBJECTIVES

- Identify key parts of the Word 2016 interface
- Open and close existing documents
- Start new documents
- Navigate in a document using scroll bars and the keyboard
- Search for help with Word
- Exit Word

📂 Project: Exploring Word

Jasmine Morales will attend Central Community College in the fall, and she wants to learn Word 2016 to help with her school assignments. She just got a new laptop with Word 2016, and she's ready to explore the Word window.

She finds that Word's Ribbon interface is intuitive and easy to use.

Jasmine decides to practice using Word 2016 by manipulating a product brochure she received as an email attachment from a friend who owns a gardening store. When she opens the file, the Compatibility Mode indicator in the title bar lets Jasmine know the document was created in a version of Word from 2010 or earlier.

Compatibility Mode deactivates new features that the earlier Word versions cannot handle. Jasmine has the option of leaving the brochure in the older Word format or converting it to the Word 2016 format so that all 2016 features are available in the document.

Note! Word 2013 and Word 2016 are compatible, so if you open a Word 2013 file, you will not see the Compatibility Mode indicator.

If Jasmine wants to share the document with her gardening friend who uses an old version of Word, she shouldn't convert the document. If she wants to be able to use a document created in a version of Word from 2010 or earlier and also use all of Word 2016's new features, she should convert the document.

How Suite It Is

Microsoft Office 2016 is a suite of software programs. A suite is several programs usually sold together as one package, which is less expensive than buying them individually. In this course, you will learn to work with Word, Excel, PowerPoint, and Access—four of the most popular software programs in the Office 2016 suite.

- **Word 2016:** This word-processing program allows you to create documents, such as letters and envelopes, and then make changes without having to retype all of the information. Other examples of Word documents include memos, reports, and fancy flyers.

- **Excel 2016:** A spreadsheet program makes organizing numbers and financial information and performing calculations a breeze. A budget is a good example of something you might create in a spreadsheet program. Other ideas include sales reports, billing statements, and graphs.

- **PowerPoint 2016:** Whether you are giving a presentation to your community center or your work colleagues, PowerPoint lets you produce elegant electronic slide shows with little effort. The tools built into this program help make any presentation a hit!

- **Access 2016:** Organizing very large amounts of data is how a database program shines. If you have a collection of hundreds of CDs or an extensive parts inventory, you can keep track of them in a database.

One of the great things about a software suite is that all programs share common features and a similar design. This means that once you have learned one program, you can easily learn another, and moving information between various programs in the suite is a snap.

What Is Word?

Word 2016 is the name of the word-processing program that is part of the Microsoft Office 2016 suite of programs. As with all word-processing programs, you use Word 2016 to electronically create and edit text. After creating a document, you can edit it. You can also make big changes, such as adding or deleting a couple of paragraphs in the middle of a page. When you add new text, the existing text moves out of the way to make room for it. When you delete text, the remaining text collapses to close the gap. Other editing changes, such as moving or copying text within a page or from one page to another, are also easy.

Word is also great for formatting text, and it also provides special features such as the Spelling & Grammar checker. There's even an AutoCorrect feature that can fix many mistakes for you.

The Word Start Screen

The Word Start screen is the first screen you see when you start the program. It offers you several ways to begin working. Don't be concerned if your Start screen is arranged differently from this example. You can rearrange the templates on the right side of the screen, and the appearance also depends on your screen's resolution.

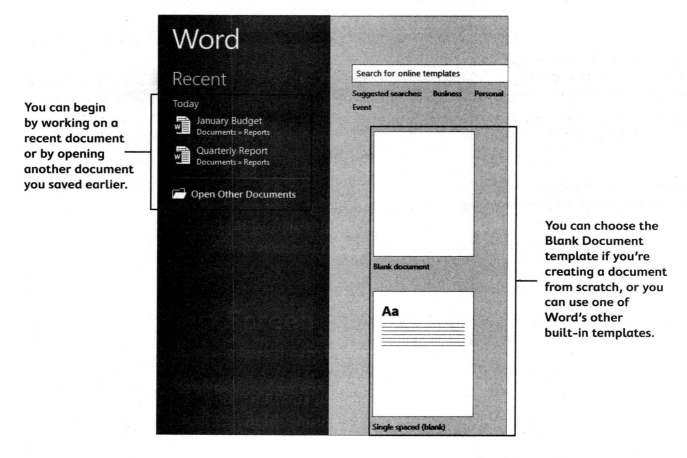

You can begin by working on a recent document or by opening another document you saved earlier.

You can choose the Blank Document template if you're creating a document from scratch, or you can use one of Word's other built-in templates.

HANDS-ON 1.1 Start Word

In this exercise, you will start the Word program.

1. If necessary, start your computer.
2. Click the **Start** ⊞ button in the bottom-left corner of the screen.
3. Scroll down the alphabetical list and click **Word 2016**.
   The Word program loads, and the Word Start screen appears.

4. **Maximize** 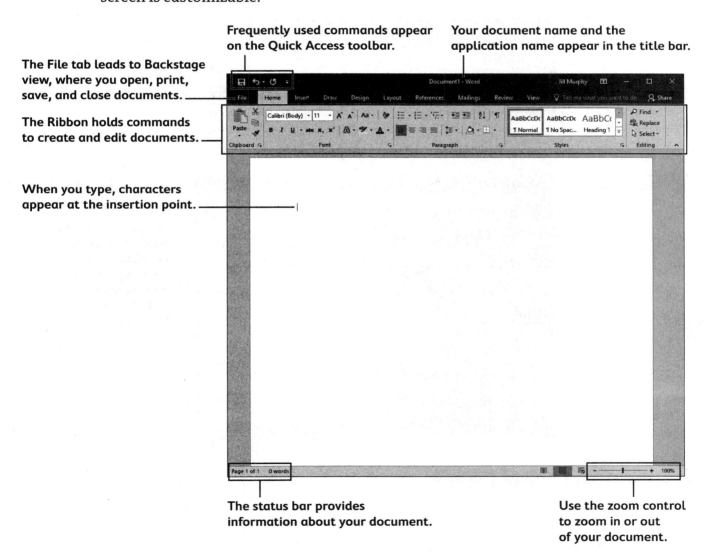 the Word window if it isn't already maximized.

5. Click the **Blank Document** template to open the Word window.

   Always leave your document open unless directed otherwise.

The Word 2016 Window

This figure describes the main elements of the Word window. Don't be concerned if your document window looks somewhat different from this illustration, as the Word screen is customizable.

Frequently used commands appear on the Quick Access toolbar.

Your document name and the application name appear in the title bar.

The File tab leads to Backstage view, where you open, print, save, and close documents.

The Ribbon holds commands to create and edit documents.

When you type, characters appear at the insertion point.

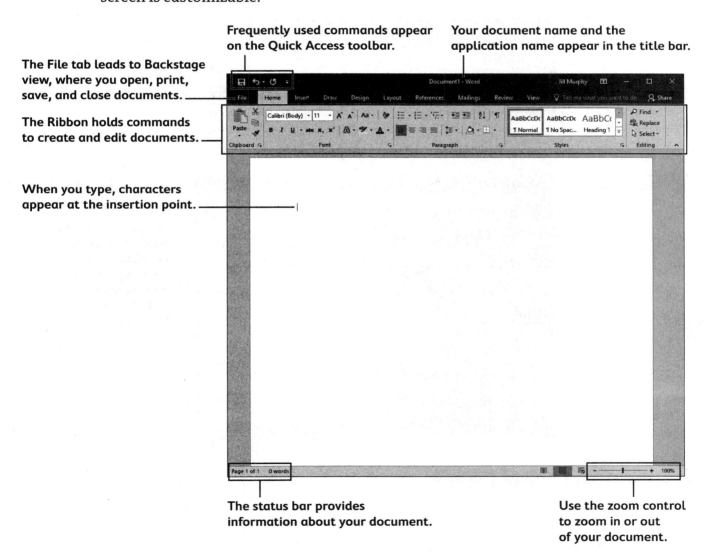

The status bar provides information about your document.

Use the zoom control to zoom in or out of your document.

The Ribbon

The band running across the top of the screen is the Ribbon. This is where you find the commands you need to create, format, and edit your documents. The Ribbon consists of three main elements:

- Tabs
- Groups
- Commands

The tabs include Home, Insert, Mailings, View, etc. A group contains related commands within a tab. Groups on the Home tab, for example, include Clipboard, Font, Paragraph, Styles, and Editing. An example of a command in the Font group is the Bold command.

Note! If you have a touch-enabled device, you may also see a Draw tab, which allows you to add notes and annotate your text by drawing on the screen.

Home tab   **Bold command button**

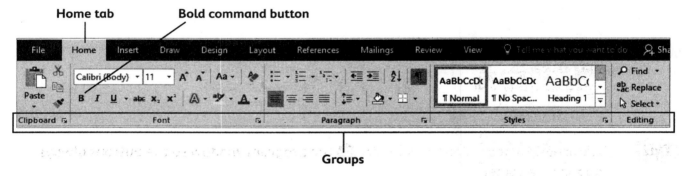

Groups

ToolTips

When you hover the mouse pointer over commands on the Ribbon, ToolTips may appear. These are little notes that contain command descriptions, and they often contain keystrokes that you can use instead of clicking commands with the mouse. In this example, you see the ToolTip for the Bold command. You can use $\boxed{\text{Ctrl}}$+$\boxed{\text{B}}$ to execute the command rather than clicking the Bold button if you wish.

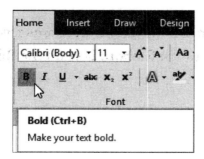

Contextual Tabs

Contextual tabs appear in context with the task you are performing. For example, if you are working with tables, the Table Tools tabs, Design and Layout, appear, as shown in the illustration on the left. If you are working with pictures, the Picture Tools' Format tab appears, as shown in the illustration on the right. You'll learn more about these tabs later in this course.

Varying Button Arrangements

The arrangement of buttons on the Ribbon can vary depending on your screen resolution and how the Word window is sized. Following are two examples of how the Paragraph group might appear on the Ribbon.

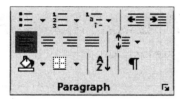 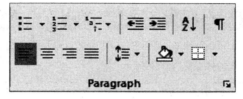

 It's usually a good idea to maximize ▢ the program window so the buttons always appear the same.

Introducing the Toolbars

There are two important toolbars in Word 2016: the Quick Access toolbar and the Mini toolbar. You will work with these toolbars later in this course.

Quick Access Toolbar

The Quick Access toolbar in the upper-left corner of the screen contains frequently used commands. It operates independently from the Ribbon. Like on the Ribbon, when you hover the mouse pointer over a button, Word displays a ToolTip describing the button and offers keystroke combinations you can use instead of clicking the button.

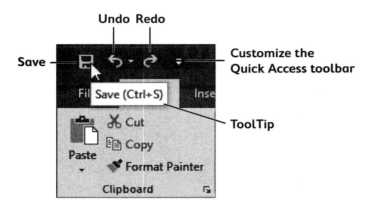

Mini Toolbar

The Mini toolbar contains frequently used formatting commands such as Bold and Italic. When you select (highlight) text, the Mini toolbar appears so you can easily format the selected text.

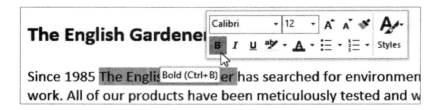

🖱 HANDS-ON 1.2 Explore Ribbon Tabs and Groups

In this exercise, you will explore various tabs and groups on the Ribbon.

1. Click the **Insert** tab to display the commands available in that category.

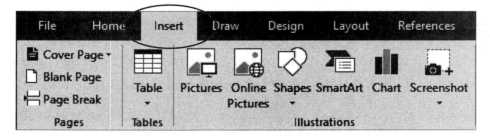

Notice the Pages, Tables, and Illustrations groups on the Insert tab.

2. Click the **Layout** tab.

This tab displays commands for arranging text on the page.

3. Feel free to examine more tabs on the Ribbon.

4. Click the **Home** tab.

Opening Documents

The Open command on the File tab displays the Open screen in Backstage view. Choose the basic location from the center panel. For example, if you want to open a document from your local computer, double-click the This PC icon. This displays the open dialog box, and you can navigate to your file storage location from there.

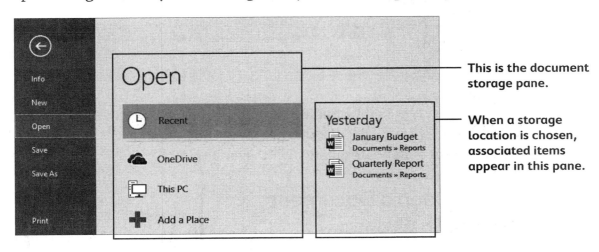

This is the document storage pane.

When a storage location is chosen, associated items appear in this pane.

The Open window in Backstage view

Opening Older Word Documents

If you open a document created in a previous version of Word, it opens in Compatibility Mode. The term appears in the title bar, as shown below. Older Word documents do not understand the new features in Word 2016, so those features are limited or disabled.

When an older document is open, a Convert command can be found in Backstage view. Use it to upgrade the file and enable the new features available in Office 2016 applications. The convert process overwrites the original file.

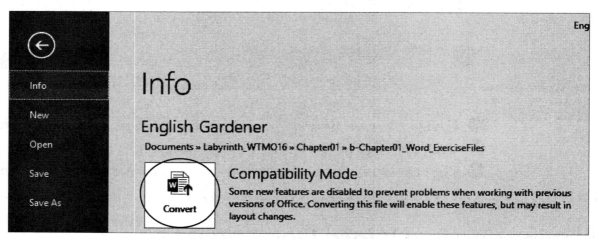

Note! When opening files in this course, if a yellow bar appears across the top of the window, which indicates a Security Warning or that the file was opened in Protected View, click Enable Content or Enable Editing (whichever displays).

HANDS-ON 1.3 Open a Document

In this exercise, you will open an existing document through the Open dialog box.

Before You Begin: Navigate to the Student Resource Center at labyrinthelab.com/wtmo16 to download the student exercise files for this book.

1. Click the **File** tab at the left end of the Ribbon and the Open screen is visible in Backstage view.

2. In the Open screen, choose your file storage location, such as This PC, from the center panel.

   You may need to consult with your instructor to determine how to navigate to your file storage location.

3. Follow these steps to open the English Gardener document:

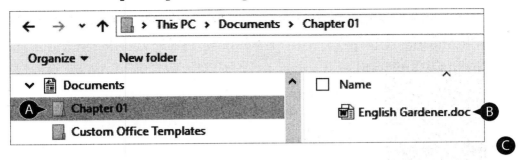

A Navigate to your file storage location and open your **Chapter 01** folder.

B Click the **English Gardener** filename to select it.

C Click the **Open** button in the bottom-right corner of the dialog box.

Navigating in a Word Document

If you are working in a multipage document, it's helpful to know about the various techniques you can use to move through documents. You can navigate using the scroll bar located at the right side of the screen, or you can use keystrokes.

The Scroll Bar

The scroll bar lets you browse through documents; however, scrolling does not move the insertion point. After scrolling, you must click in the document where you want to reposition the insertion point.

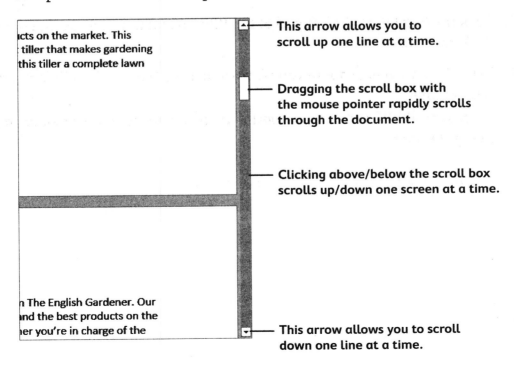

This arrow allows you to scroll up one line at a time.

Dragging the scroll box with the mouse pointer rapidly scrolls through the document.

Clicking above/below the scroll box scrolls up/down one screen at a time.

This arrow allows you to scroll down one line at a time.

Different Mouse Pointer Shapes

The mouse pointer must be shaped like an I-beam ⅠＩ when you want to position the flashing insertion point using the mouse. (You click the left mouse button to place the insertion point at the position of the I-beam.) The mouse pointer appears as an I-beam when positioned between the document margins.

The mouse pointer appears as a white, right-tilting arrow ⬚ when in the selection bar, which is located in the document's left margin. The white arrow is used to select (highlight) text. You will learn more about selecting text later in this course.

HANDS-ON 1.4 Scroll and Position the Insertion Point

In this exercise, you will use the scroll bar to move through a document. Then you will reposition the insertion point in the document.

1. Follow these steps to scroll within the document:

   Ⓐ Click the **scroll down** button five times.

   Ⓑ Click the **scroll up** button five times to move in the other direction.

   Notice that the flashing insertion point does not move when you use the scroll bar.

2. Position the **I-beam** ⅠＩ mouse pointer in the body of the document.

   The mouse pointer looks like an I-beam when it's between the document margins.

3. Click the **I-beam** ⅠＩ mouse pointer anywhere in the document to position the flashing insertion point.

   If the background is highlighted, you accidentally dragged the mouse pointer and selected the text. Deselect by clicking the mouse pointer in the document background and try again.

4. Move the mouse pointer into the left margin area.

   The white arrow ⬚ shape is now visible.

5. In the first paragraph, position the **I-beam** ⅠＩ mouse pointer in the first line and click.

   The insertion point appears just where you clicked.

6. Click the open part of the **scroll bar** below the scroll box to move down one screen.

7. Drag the **scroll box** down with the mouse pointer until the end of the document is visible.

8. Click the **I-beam** $\boxed{I}$ mouse pointer at the end of the text to position the insertion point on the last page.

9. Drag the **scroll box** to the top of the scroll bar and then click the **I-beam** $\boxed{I}$ mouse pointer in front of the first word of the first paragraph.

The Keyboard

Whether you use the mouse or the keyboard to navigate through a document is a matter of personal preference. Navigating with the keyboard always moves the insertion point so it will be with you when you arrive at your destination. The following table provides keystrokes that allow you to move quickly through a document.

KEYBOARD NAVIGATION TECHNIQUES

Press	To Move
$\boxed{\rightarrow}$	One character to the right
$\boxed{\leftarrow}$	One character to the left
$\boxed{Ctrl}+\boxed{\rightarrow}$	One word to the right
$\boxed{Ctrl}+\boxed{\leftarrow}$	One word to the left
$\boxed{\downarrow}$	Down one line
$\boxed{\uparrow}$	Up one line
$\boxed{Page\ Down}$	Down one screen
$\boxed{Page\ Up}$	Up one screen
$\boxed{Ctrl}+\boxed{End}$	To the end of the document
$\boxed{Ctrl}+\boxed{Home}$	To the beginning of the document
$\boxed{End}$	To the end of the line
$\boxed{Home}$	To the beginning of the line

🖰 HANDS-ON 1.5 Navigate with the Keyboard

In this exercise, you will use the keyboard to move through a document.

1. Click the **I-beam** I mouse pointer in the middle of the first line of the second paragraph.

2. Tap the **right arrow** → and **left arrow** ← keys a few times to move to the right and left, one character at a time.

3. Tap the **up arrow** ↑ and the **down arrow** ↓ keys a few times to move up and down, one line at a time.

4. Hold down Ctrl and keep it down, and then tap Home to move to the beginning of the document. Release Ctrl.

5. Use the arrow keys to position the insertion point in the middle of the first line of the first paragraph.

6. Hold down Ctrl and keep it down, and then tap the **left arrow** ← key a few times to move to the left, one word at a time. Release Ctrl.

7. Hold down Ctrl and keep it down, and then tap the **right arrow** → key several times to move to the right, one word at a time. Release Ctrl.

8. Tap Home to move to the beginning of the line.

9. Tap End to move to the end of the line.

10. Tap Page Down and Page Up to scroll down and up, one screen at a time.

· ·

Closing Documents

You close a file by clicking the File tab and choosing the Close command from the panel on the left in Backstage view.

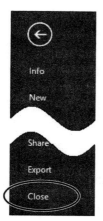

If you haven't saved your document, Word will prompt you to save it.

 HANDS-ON 1.6 **Close the Document**

In this exercise, you will close your file.

1. Click the **File** tab and choose **Close** from the panel on the left.

2. Click **Don't Save** if Word asks if you want to save changes.

3. If a blank document is on the screen, use the same technique to close it.
   The document window below the Ribbon is completely blank when all documents are closed.

Starting a New, Blank Document

You can start a new, blank document by clicking the File tab and choosing the New command from the panel on the left in Backstage view. This opens the New screen, where you can click the Blank Document template to start a new document.

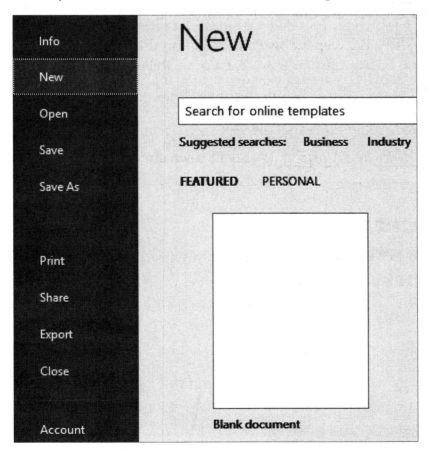

You can also open a new document using the keyboard shortcut Ctrl + N.

QUICK REFERENCE: Opening, Closing, and Starting a New Document

Task	Procedure
Open a document	▪ Click the File tab, choose Open, and navigate to your file storage location. ▪ Click the desired file, and then click the Open button.
Close a document	▪ Click the File tab and choose Close.
Start a new document	▪ Click the File tab and choose New, and then click the Blank Document template. Alternatively, press Ctrl + N.

HANDS-ON 1.7 Start a New Document

In this exercise, you will open a new, blank document. No documents should be open in the Word window.

1. Click the **File** tab and choose **New** from the left-hand panel.

2. Click the **Blank Document** template to start a new document.
   Now you will close this new document and use the shortcut keystrokes to start another one.

3. Click the **File** tab and choose **Close** from the left-hand panel.

4. Hold down the Ctrl key and tap the N key on your keyboard.
   Leave the document open.

· ·

Getting Help in Word

Help in Word 2016 is available in two main modes:

▪ The Tell Me What You Want to Do box

▪ The Help window

The Tell Me What You Want to Do box appears at the top of the Word window, to the right of the Ribbon tabs.

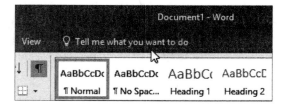

Click in the box and type your question or the name of the feature you are looking for. You will see a list of search results; click the option you want, and Word Help will take you to that feature.

You can access the Help window directly by clicking the question mark located at the top right of the screen in Backstage view.

Tip! Tapping the $\boxed{F1}$ function key at the top of your keyboard also opens the Help window.

HANDS-ON 1.8 Use Word Help

In this exercise, you will work with different help techniques.

1. Click the **Tell Me What You Want to Do** box at the top of the Word window.

2. Type: **print**

   A list of search results appears.

3. Choose **Print Preview and Print** from the list.

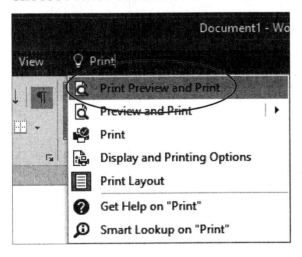

Word takes you to the Print screen in Backstage view, where you can preview and print the document.

4. Click the **question mark** in the upper-right corner of the Print screen to open the Help window.

5. Type **print** in the search box and then choose **print** from the search results list.

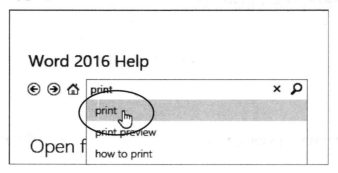

6. In the next window, click **Print a Document in Word**.

Print a document in Word

Print a document in Word 2016 for Windows. Before you print, it's a good idea to preview your document to make sure that it looks the way you want.

7. Scroll through the steps for printing a document.

You'll work with printing later in the course, so this gives you a glimpse into the future.

8. Click the **Close** ☒ button in the upper-right corner of the Help window.

9. Click the **Back** ◉ button in the upper-left corner of the Backstage view window.

Exiting Word

You exit Word and other Office 2016 applications by clicking the Close ■ button in the upper-right corner of the window. If you have more than one document open, you need to close each document. It's important to exit your application in an orderly fashion, as turning off your computer before exiting could cause you to lose data.

HANDS-ON 1.9 Exit Word

In this exercise, you will exit Word. Since you haven't made any changes to your document, you won't bother saving it.

1. Click the **Close** ■ button in the upper-right corner of the Word window.

2. If you are prompted to save your changes, click the **Don't Save** button.

3. If you have more than one document open, close any remaining documents without saving.

Word closes, and the Windows Desktop appears.

Self-Assessment

Check your knowledge of this chapter's key concepts and skills by completing the Self-Assessment.

Page number

1. The insertion point automatically repositions when you navigate using the scroll bars.   **true   false**   _____

2. The mouse pointer looks like a white arrow when placed in the left margin of a document.   **true   false**   _____

3. The Quick Access toolbar contains commands for positioning the insertion point.   **true   false**   _____

4. The button arrangement on the Ribbon can vary depending on how the Word window is sized.   **true   false**   _____

5. The File tab provides access to file-management tasks, such as document saving, opening, and closing.   **true   false**   _____

6. The commands needed to create and edit documents are provided on the Ribbon.   **true   false**   _____

7. Which shape does the mouse pointer have when it is in the text area?

   A. Right-tilting arrow

   B. I-beam

   C. Left-tilting arrow

   D. Four-headed arrow

   Page number: _____

8. The Open dialog box is where you can _____.

   A. save newly created documents

   B. convert documents created in older Word versions to Word 2016

   C. start a new, blank document

   D. navigate to and open previously saved documents

   Page number: _____

9. The Ribbon consists of which of the following three primary areas?

   A. Tabs, groups, and the selection bar

   B. The Quick Access toolbar, commands, and groups

   C. Tabs, groups, and commands

   D. The Quick Access toolbar, the status bar, and groups

   Page number: _____

10. When you add text to a document, _____.

   A. the existing text moves out of the way to make room for it

   B. the mouse pointer is shaped like a white arrow

   C. the Mini toolbar appears in case you want to format text

   D. the existing text collapses to close the gap

   Page number: _____

Skill Builders

SKILL BUILDER 1.1 Identify Elements of the Word 2016 Window

In this exercise, you will name parts of the Word window. It's important to use the correct terms when talking about the Word program; for example, if you need to discuss an issue with people in your IT department, they can help you faster if they are clear on what you are talking about.

1. Start **Word 2016** and click the **Blank Document** template.

2. In the table provided at the end of this exercise, write the correct terms for items A–G.

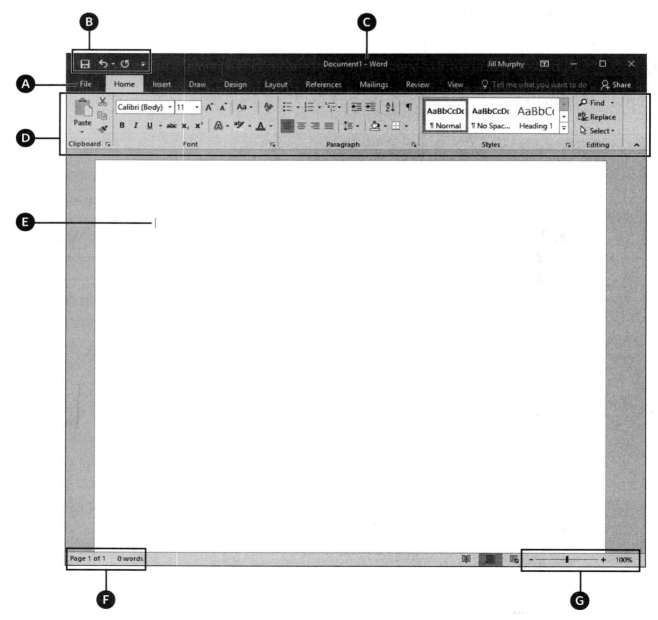

Letter	Term
A	
B	
C	
D	
E	
F	
G	

· ·

SKILL BUILDER 1.2 Use Word Help

In this exercise, you will use the Word Help window to find information that can assist you as you work.

1. Tap the F1 key at the top of your keyboard to open the Help window.

2. Type **keyboard shortcuts** in the search box and then choose **keyboard shortcuts** from the search results list.

3. In the next window, click the **Keyboard Shortcuts for Microsoft Word 2016 for Windows** link, and in the next window, click the **Frequently Used Shortcuts** link.

   Notice the shortcuts for some features you used in this chapter are at the top of the list.

4. Take a moment to scroll through the list and then click the **Close** ☒ button in the upper-right corner of the Help window.

· ·

SKILL BUILDER 1.3 Navigate in Word

In this exercise, you will use a report you created for your Southeast Asian Languages class to practice navigating in Word.

1. Click the **File** tab and choose **Open** from the left-hand panel.

2. Choose your main storage device, which will likely be **This PC** ▣.

3. If necessary, navigate to your file storage location and open your **Chapter 01** folder.

4. Double-click the file named **sb-Heart Report** to open it.

5. Click the **scroll bar** below the scroll box to move down a screen.

6. Position the insertion point in the middle of the first line on page 2.

7. Drag the **scroll box** to the top of the document and position the insertion point at the beginning of the document.

8. Click the **Scroll Down** ⊡ button and hold the mouse button down for a few seconds to scroll quickly through the document.

9. Drag the **scroll box** back to the top of the scroll bar.

Navigate with the Keyboard

If you press and hold the arrow keys, the insertion point moves quickly through the document.

10. Press and hold the **down arrow** ↓ key enough times to position the insertion point in the first line of the first paragraph on the second page.

11. Tap End to move the insertion point to the end of the line.

12. Tap Home to move to the beginning of the line.

13. Press Ctrl + End to place the insertion point at the end of the document.

14. Press Ctrl + Home to move to the top of the document.

15. Press and hold the ↓ key long enough to move the insertion point to the first line of the first paragraph on the second page.

16. Hold down Ctrl and tap → three times to move to the right, one word at a time.

Close the Document and Exit Word

17. Click the **File** tab and choose **Close** from the left-hand panel.

18. Click **Don't Save** if a message appears asking if you want to save changes.

19. Click **Close** ✕ in the upper-right corner of the Word window.

Writing a Letter and a Résumé

The business letter is one of the most common business documents. In this chapter, you will lay out a professional-looking letter and work with techniques and features that will make your letter stand out from the crowd. Then you will use Word's table feature to create a well-organized, eye-catching résumé. Finally, you will print your documents and create an envelope for mailing your letter and résumé.

LEARNING OBJECTIVES

- Work with spacing and AutoComplete
- Use Word Wrap and the Enter key to lay out paragraphs
- Use bullet points and create a table
- Save and print documents
- Type an envelope

📂 Project: Crafting a Cover Letter and a Résumé

Victor Gomez just completed his degree in sales and marketing. He is now ready to begin his career! He is interested in applying for a Customer Support position at Goodspeed Industries. Using Word 2016, Victor creates a professional-looking cover letter and uses Word's Bullets feature to point out pertinent information he wants to draw the hiring manager's attention to. He then uses a table to organize his résumé.

February 10, 2016

Mr. Anthony Williams, Hiring Manager
Goodspeed Industries
456 Apple Blossom Lane
Windy Hills, CA 94941

Dear Mr. Williams:

Your ad for a Customer Support Representative in this Sunday's Chronicle caught my attention. I believe I can offer Goodspeed Industries a blend of skills and enthusiasm that will help you maintain a satisfied client base.

- Principles of good salesmanship and clear, effective communication skills have been the focus of my studies during the last four years.
- A double major in Sales and Communications demonstrates that I can take on above-average challenges and responsibilities. I am not afraid of hard work, which is demonstrated by my 3.9 grade point average.
- The positions I have held in student government demonstrate my leadership abilities and my interest in people's needs and challenges.
- To finance my education, I worked in a hospi[tal] quickly gain rapport and to efficiently assist p[eople]

I am excited about starting my professional career, a[nd] Goodspeed Industries' success. I will call you in the n[ext]

Best regards,

Victor Gomez

Enclosure

Victor Gomez
123 Cherry Blossom Lane
Windy Hills, CA 94941
415-555-1212
victor@yahoo.com

Objective	A challenging career where I can use my sales and communications skills
Qualifications	<ul><li>Proven ability to close sales</li><li>Superb communications and presentation skills</li><li>Ability to quickly gain client rapport</li></ul>
Education	<ul><li>B.S. Sales and Marketing, Windy Hills University, 2016</li><li>B.S. Communications, Windy Hills University, 2016</li><li>3.9 Grade Point Average</li></ul>
Computer Skills	<ul><li>Microsoft Word, Excel, PowerPoint, and Access</li><li>Contact Management Software</li></ul>
Work Experience	<ul><li>Waiter, family restaurant, summers during high school</li><li>Customer Support Assistant, Windy Hills Community Hospital, summers and weekends during college</li></ul>
Student Government	<ul><li>Student Body President, Senior Year</li><li>Class President, Junior Year</li><li>Student Council, Membership Coordinator, Sophomore Year</li></ul>

Typing a Cover Letter

In this part of the chapter, you will type a cover letter. Later you will create a résumé and an envelope.

Tip! If you google *cover letter,* you will find many websites that provide good ideas for cover letters designed to grab the attention of a hiring manager.

Text is always typed at the flashing insertion point; therefore, you must position the insertion point at the desired location before typing. As you type, the insertion point moves along in front of the text.

Line and Paragraph Spacing

The default line spacing in Word 2016 is 1.08 rather than 1.0. This adds an extra 8% more space between lines than regular single spacing. It also adds 8 points of space after paragraphs. Therefore, rather than tapping Enter twice at the end of a paragraph, you just tap Enter once and Word adds the extra spacing.

When you choose the Blank Document template on the Word Start screen or on the New screen in Backstage view, you are using the default 1.08 spacing.

Some documents typically require single spacing, such as business letters, reports, and proposals. Word offers these methods for applying single spacing:

- Single Spaced (blank) template

- Line and Paragraph Spacing button

Single-Spaced Template

Choosing the Single Spaced (blank) template from the Word Start screen or from the New screen in Backstage view opens a single-spaced document. This is a good choice if the majority of your document will be single spaced. If you will use single spacing in only part of your document, the Line and Paragraph Spacing button is a good choice.

Single spaced (blank)

Line and Paragraph Spacing Button

If you start a new document using 1.08 spacing and then decide you want to apply single spacing to a portion of the document, you can choose the options indicated in the following illustration. You must select (highlight) the text to be single spaced.

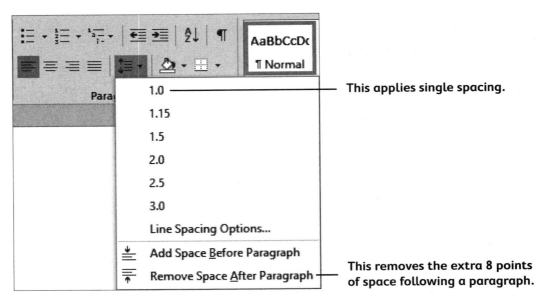

This applies single spacing.

This removes the extra 8 points of space following a paragraph.

Apply these settings when you wish to type with more compact, traditional spacing.

Another way to eliminate extra spacing at the end of a paragraph is to press Shift + Enter rather than just Enter .

Nonprinting Characters

Word has a number of nonprinting characters that are not visible unless you turn on the Show/Hide feature. Nonprinting characters do not appear on the printed page even when the characters appear on the screen. The Show/Hide button on the Ribbon displays nonprinting characters.

The Enter and Spacebar keys, as well as several others, create nonprinting characters. Being able to see these characters can help you make sure the spacing is correct in your document.

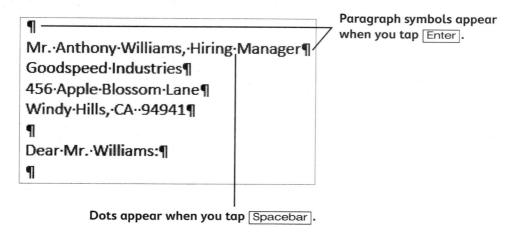

¶

Mr.·Anthony·Williams,·Hiring·Manager¶

Goodspeed·Industries¶

456·Apple·Blossom·Lane¶

Windy·Hills,·CA··94941¶

¶

Dear·Mr.·Williams:¶

¶

Paragraph symbols appear when you tap Enter .

Dots appear when you tap Spacebar .

Paragraph Symbols Carry Formatting

All new, blank documents contain a paragraph symbol that you can only see by turning on the Show/Hide feature. Paragraph symbols carry formatting in them. You can select (highlight) the paragraph symbol in a blank document and reformat it, thereby changing the default format for that document.

Note! This chapter provides a quick introduction to formatting. You will learn a lot more about formatting documents later in this course.

AutoComplete

AutoComplete can do some of your typing for you. It recognizes certain words and phrases, such as names of months and days of the week, and presents a pop-up note offering to complete them for you. You accept the term that AutoComplete proposes by tapping Enter .

November (Press ENTER to Insert)

Nove

When you tap Enter , if it's the current month, Word will complete the current date for you.

If you don't want to accept AutoComplete's suggestion, just keep typing, and the pop-up note will disappear.

🖱 HANDS-ON 2.1 Set Up a Document

In this exercise, you will display nonprinting characters, select (highlight) the embedded paragraph symbol, change the default line spacing to 1.0, and remove additional space after the paragraph. Then you will use AutoComplete to insert the date.

1. Start **Word** and choose the **Blank Document** template.
2. **Maximize** ☐ the Word window if it isn't already maximized.
3. Follow these steps to turn on the Show/Hide feature:

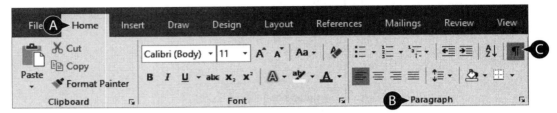

- **A** If necessary, click the **Home** tab.
- **B** Locate the **Paragraph** group.
- **C** Click the **Show/Hide** button.

A paragraph symbol is now visible on the page.

Note! Later in this book, such steps will be written as "Choose Home→Paragraph→ Show/Hide ¶."

4. Follow these steps to select (highlight) the paragraph symbol:

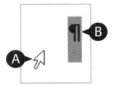

- **A** Position the mouse pointer, which will appear as a white, right-tilting arrow, in the margin to the left of the paragraph symbol.
- **B** Click the left mouse button to select the paragraph symbol.

5. Choose **Home→Paragraph→Line and Paragraph Spacing** 📝.

6. Follow these steps to change the line spacing and remove the extra space after a paragraph:

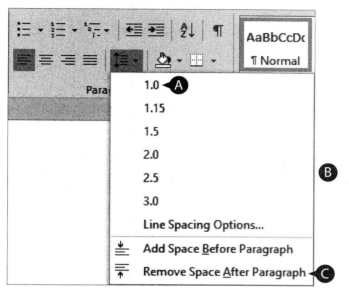

Ⓐ Choose **1.0** (single spacing).

Ⓑ Click the **Line and Paragraph Spacing** button again.

Step A closed the menu, so now you must reopen it.

Ⓒ Choose **Remove Space After Paragraph**.

Now you will enter the date using AutoComplete.

7. Tap Enter six times to place the insertion point about 2 inches from the top of the page.

8. Type **Febr** and stop when AutoComplete displays a pop-up note.

AutoComplete suggests the word it thinks you are typing and offers to complete it.

9. Tap Enter to automatically insert *February* into the letter.

10. Finish typing the date as **February 10, 2016**.

If you make a typo, use Backspace or Delete to erase from the left or right of the insertion point, respectively, and then continue typing. You can also click the Undo button on the Quick Access toolbar to undo mistakes, starting with the most recent error.

Always leave your document open unless directed otherwise.

The Enter Key and Word Wrap

Tap the Enter key at the end of a short line that must remain short. The greeting line in a letter is a good example; it consists of a short line:

Dear Mr. Williams: Enter

You also use the Enter key whenever you need to create blank lines, such as between paragraphs.

When NOT to Use the Enter Key

When you type along a line and reach the right-hand margin, Word automatically wraps down to the next line. You *should not* tap Enter at the ends of lines *within* a paragraph. If you do, it can make your life very difficult when it is time to make editing changes. Just let it wrap!

Tip! As you complete the exercises in this chapter, the text on your screen may not begin a new line at the same location as the illustrations show. Don't be concerned; just let the text wrap at the end of the line. Use Enter only where indicated.

HANDS-ON 2.2 Use the Enter Key and Word Wrap

In this exercise, you will use Enter to create blank lines and to force the inside address lines and the greeting line to remain short. You'll also let Word Wrap take care of the line endings in the main paragraphs.

Don't be concerned if you see squiggly red or blue underlines. They indicate possible spelling or grammatical errors, which you'll learn more about later. If you know you made a typo, just use Backspace or Delete to delete it and keep typing.

1. Tap Enter four times to generate white space after the date.
   Word inserts a fresh line each time you tap Enter.

2. Type this inside address and greeting line, tapping Enter where indicated:
   Mr. Anthony Williams, Hiring Manager Enter
   Goodspeed Industries Enter
   456 Apple Blossom Lane Enter
   Windy Hills, CA 94941 Enter
   Enter
   Dear Mr. Williams: Enter
   Enter

3. Type this paragraph, but don't tap ⎡Enter⎤ until indicated at the end of the paragraph.

Don't be concerned if your line widths are not the same as that shown here. Word Wrap will take care of the line endings.

```
Your ad for a Customer Support Representative in this
Sunday's paper caught my attention. I believe I can offer
Goodspeed Industries a blend of skills and enthusiasm that
will help you maintain a satisfied client base. ⎡Enter⎤
```

The Bullets Feature

Using bullet points makes it easy for your reader to find pertinent information in your document. If you are writing to busy people, such as hiring managers, they will appreciate bullets that focus their attention on the significant points. You can use the Bullets feature located in the Paragraph group of the Home tab to quickly create bulleted lists.

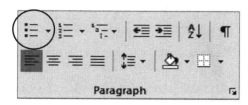

Once you begin a bulleted list, tapping ⎡Enter⎤ generates the next bullet. When you have completed the list, tap ⎡Enter⎤ twice to turn off the feature.

HANDS-ON 2.3 Create a Bulleted List

In this exercise, you will use bullets to draw the hiring manager's attention to the specific traits and accomplishments that should be called out in the cover letter.

1. Choose **Home→Paragraph→Bullets** ⬚.

2. Type this paragraph:

```
Principles of good salesmanship and clear, effective
communication skills have been the focus of my studies
during the last four years.
```

3. Tap ⎡Enter⎤ to generate the next bullet.

4. Type these bulleted paragraphs, tapping `Enter` where indicated:

- **A double major in Sales and Communications demonstrates that I can take on above-average challenges and responsibilities. I am not afraid of hard work, which is demonstrated by my 3.9 grade point average.** `Enter`

- **The positions I have held in student government demonstrate my leadership abilities and my interest in people's needs and challenges.** `Enter`

- **To finance my education, I worked in a hospital call center, where I demonstrated the skill to quickly gain rapport and to efficiently assist patients with their billing questions.** `Enter`

Your last `Enter` generated another bullet; a second `Enter` turns off the feature.

5. Tap `Enter` again.

Now you're ready to finish the letter.

6. Type this paragraph and closing:

I am excited about starting my professional career, and I would appreciate the opportunity to add to Goodspeed Industries' success. I will call you in the near future to see if we can schedule a time to meet. `Enter`
`Enter`
Best regards, `Enter`
`Enter`
`Enter`
`Enter`
Victor Gomez `Enter`
`Enter`

Saving a Document

When you are working on a document, it is located in your computer's memory. Memory is *temporary* storage, meaning that if you lose power, your computer loses its memory. If this happens, you could lose information.

To avoid this problem, save your letter on a storage device, such as a USB drive or the hard drive inside your computer. These storage methods are permanent, meaning your data won't be lost in the event of a power failure. You should save frequently— every five to ten minutes is a good idea.

Save Versus Save As

In Word, you can save a document by issuing one of two commands: Save or Save As. The first time you save a document, you use the Save As command. After that, when you make modifications to a document, you use the Save command to update the file in your storage device.

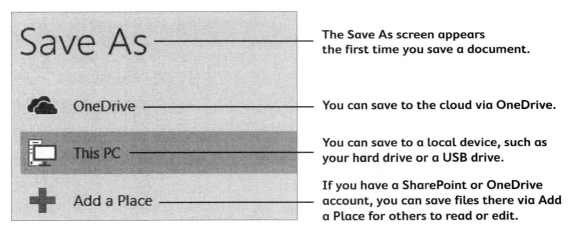

The Save As screen appears the first time you save a document.

You can save to the cloud via OneDrive.

You can save to a local device, such as your hard drive or a USB drive.

If you have a SharePoint or OneDrive account, you can save files there via Add a Place for others to read or edit.

Note! Storing documents in OneDrive is beyond the scope of this course. You will save your files on a local device.

After choosing a location in the Save As screen, the Save As dialog box opens. This is where you navigate to your file storage location and name and save the file.

You choose your file storage location here. ———

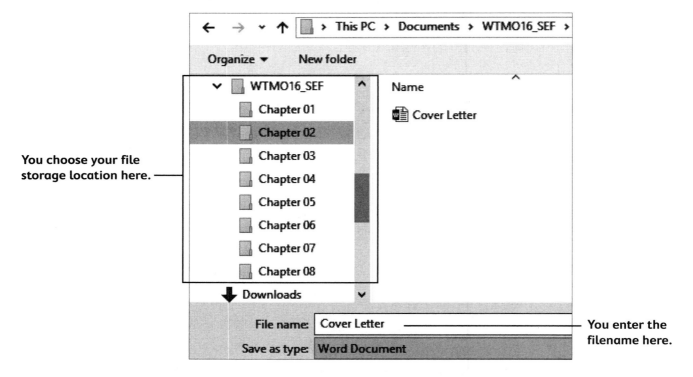

You enter the filename here.

 Tip! You can even save a document created in Word 2016 down to an earlier document format in order to share a file with someone who uses Word 2003 (or even earlier!).

HANDS-ON 2.4 Save Your Cover Letter

In this exercise, you will save the cover letter you've been creating. This way, if there is a power failure, your letter will not be lost.

1. Choose **File→Save As** to display the Save As screen in Backstage view.

2. Double-click the **This PC** icon to open the Save As dialog box.

3. Follow these steps to save your document:

Your Save As dialog box may contain different files and folders than those shown here.

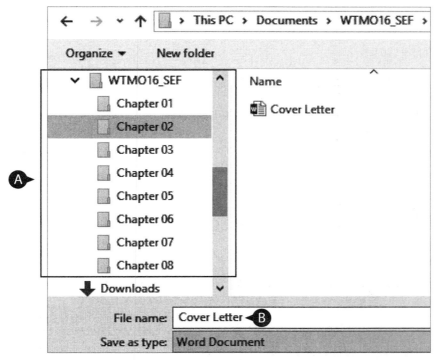

Ⓐ Use the Navigation pane to locate and open your **Chapter 02** folder.

Ⓑ Word always proposes a filename. Replace it with: `Cover Letter`

4. Click the **Save** button in the bottom-right corner of the dialog box.

Saving a Modified Document

The first time you save a document, you give it a name. If you make changes to the document after that, you must save it again so the changes are not lost. Once the document is saved and named, you can use the Save command rather than the Save As command.

You can use the Save button on the Quick Access toolbar or the Save command in Backstage view to save a modified document. When you use Save versus Save As, no dialog box appears; the saving happens in the background.

Task	Procedure
Save a document for the first time	<ul><li>Choose File→Save As.</li><li>Double-click an option (such as This PC) in the document storage pane and then navigate to your storage location.</li><li>Type the filename and click Save.</li></ul>
Save a modified document	<ul><li>Choose File→Save or click Save on the Quick Access toolbar.</li></ul>

HANDS-ON 2.5 Modify Your Letter and Resave

In this exercise, you will add the enclosure notification to the bottom of the letter to notify the reader to check for an additional document in the envelope. Later in this chapter, you will create a résumé, which will be the enclosure.

1. If necessary, choose **Home→Paragraph→Show/Hide** ¶ to display nonprinting characters.
   Feel free to turn this feature on and off as you prefer.

2. Position the insertion point at the bottom of the letter.
   Now you will add the enclosure notification to the letter. There should be a blank line separating the enclosure notification from the signature block.

3. If necessary, tap [Enter] to place the insertion point on the second blank line below the signature block.

4. Type the word: **Enclosure**
   Now you'll save the letter again to save the change you just made.

5. Click the **Save** button on the Quick Access toolbar in the upper-left corner of the Word window.

Printing Documents

You can print your document by choosing Print in the left-hand panel in Backstage view. Choosing Print opens the printer controls in the center panel (shown at left in the illustration) and a preview of your letter in the right-hand panel.

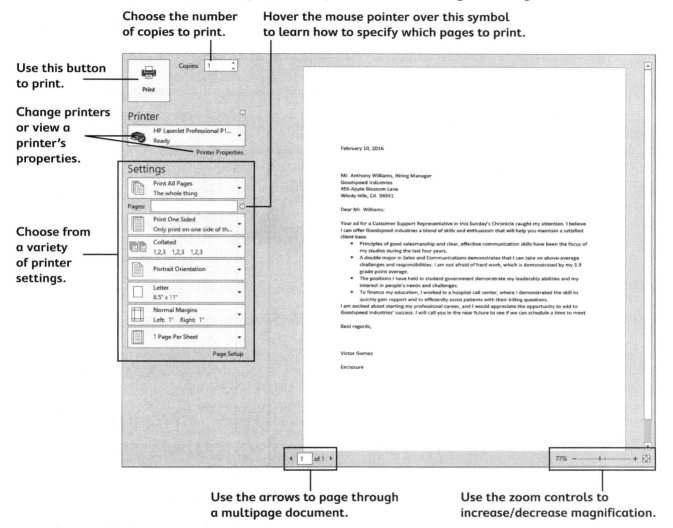

Choose the number of copies to print.

Hover the mouse pointer over this symbol to learn how to specify which pages to print.

Use this button to print.

Change printers or view a printer's properties.

Choose from a variety of printer settings.

Use the arrows to page through a multipage document.

Use the zoom controls to increase/decrease magnification.

HANDS-ON 2.6 Print Your Cover Letter

In this exercise, you will preview your letter to see how it looks *before* you print. Then you will print the file.

1. Choose **File→Print**.

2. Drag the **zoom controls slider** in the bottom-right corner of the preview panel a few times to zoom in and out of the letter.

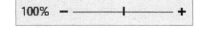

3. Click the **Zoom to Page** button to the right of the zoom controls to fit the page to the preview panel.

4. At the top of the Backstage view center panel, click the top part of the **spin box** once to change the number of copies to **2**.

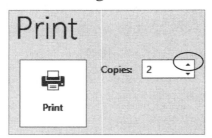

5. Click **Print** at the top of the center panel to print two copies of your letter.

6. Choose **File**→**Close** to close your cover letter.

Use Word Tables to Organize a Résumé

A table is one of Word's most useful tools. It allows you to present data in columns and rows. Tables provide a powerful means of communicating information, yet they are flexible and easy to use. In this part of the chapter, you will use a table to create a résumé.

Tip! If you google *résumé*, you will find helpful guidelines for creating a résumé that's targeted to the job you are applying for.

Using the Table button on the Insert tab allows you to create a new table.

You can drag the mouse pointer to select the desired number of columns and rows. The indicator shows your table dimensions (4×3) at the top of the table grid.

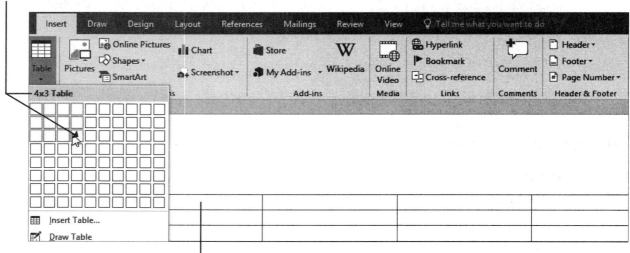

Word's Live Preview feature shows what the table will look like before you insert it.

The rectangles that make up the table are referred to as *cells*.

Merging Cells and Centering Data in Cells

Frequently, the first row of a table contains a title describing the contents of the table. In the case of a résumé, it's likely the first row would contain the job applicant's contact information. Merging the cells and centering the information within the merged cell gives your résumé a polished look.

Victor Gomez	
123 Cherry Blossom Lane	
Windy Hills, CA 94941	
415-555-1212	
victor@yahoo.com	
Objective	A challenging career where I can use my sales and communications skills
Qualifications	• Proven ability to close sales • Superb communications and presentation skills • Ability to quickly gain client rapport

Table Tools Contextual Tabs: Design and Layout

Contextual tabs appear in context with the task you are performing. You will use the Table Tools' contextual Layout tab to merge and center align the first row of the table.

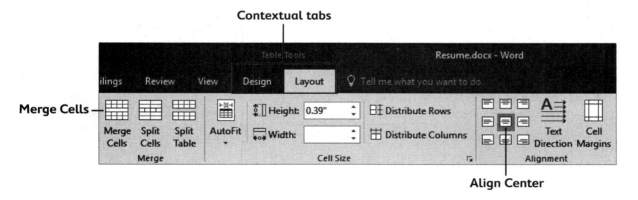

Contextual tabs

Merge Cells

Align Center

✋ HANDS-ON 2.7 Create a Table for Your Résumé

In this exercise, you will create a table to hold the résumé content. You'll also merge and center-align the cells in the first row to ready it for contact information.

1. Choose **File→New**.

2. Click the **Blank Document** template to open a new document.

3. Tap [Enter] four times so the table will be well positioned vertically on the page.

4. Choose **Insert→Tables→Table** ⊞.

5. Follow these steps to create a two-column, seven-row table:

Remember, if you make a mistake, just click Undo ↩ on the Quick Access toolbar.

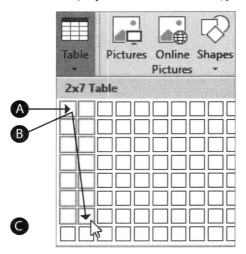

Ⓐ Position the mouse pointer in the upper-left corner of the grid, hold down the mouse button, and drag to the right to select two columns. Do not release the mouse button.

Ⓑ Drag the mouse pointer down to the seventh row.

Ⓒ Release the mouse button.

A 2×7 table appears in your document. Now you will merge and center cells in preparation for entering contact information.

6. Follow these steps to merge and center the first row of the table:

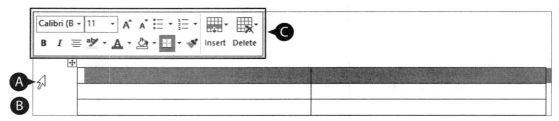

Ⓐ Position the mouse pointer, which will show as a white, right-tilting arrow, in the margin and to the left of the table's first row.

Ⓑ Click the mouse button to select (highlight) the first row.

Ⓒ Notice the Mini toolbar, which appears whenever you select text or table rows or columns in Word. Ignore it for now; it will fade away.

Notice the Table Tools with the Design and Layout contextual tabs that now appear on the Ribbon. They will appear whenever your table is active.

7. Choose **Table Tools→Layout→Merge→Merge Cells** 🟦.

8. Choose **Table Tools→Layout→Alignment→Align Center** ▣.

If necessary, hover the mouse pointer over the alignment buttons on the left side of the Alignment group to display their ToolTips. Now when you type in the first row, the text will be center aligned.

9. Click anywhere else in the table to deselect the first row.

Save Your File

10. Choose **File→Save As** to display the Save As screen in Backstage view.

11. Double-click the **This PC** 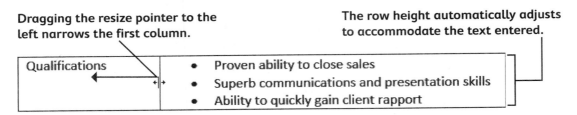 icon to open the Save As dialog box.

12. Navigate to your **Chapter 02** folder and notice that Word proposes a name in the File Name field at the bottom of the dialog box.
    You can replace the name that Word is proposing.

13. Delete the proposed name and type **Resume** in its place.

14. Click the **Save** button in the bottom-right corner of the dialog box.

Navigating in Tables and Adding Rows

You can position the insertion point in a cell simply by clicking it. However, it's often more efficient to use the keyboard to move among cells. You use the Tab key to move forward one cell and Shift + Tab to move back one cell. If the insertion point is in the last cell of the table, tapping Tab adds a new row to the bottom of the table.

Resizing Column Widths and Row Heights

Using the Table button grid to create a table inserts equally spaced columns. In many instances, such as when typing a résumé, you might prefer to vary column widths. Word's Table feature makes changing column widths a snap. Row heights adjust automatically to fit the text you enter. The resize pointer appears when you place the mouse pointer on a column gridline. You can then adjust the column width by dragging the gridline left or right.

Dragging the resize pointer to the left narrows the first column.

The row height automatically adjusts to accommodate the text entered.

Qualifications	• Proven ability to close sales
	• Superb communications and presentation skills
	• Ability to quickly gain client rapport

Note! Make sure no cells are selected (highlighted) when you drag the column gridline. Otherwise, you might change the width of the selected cells only.

HANDS-ON 2.8 Fill in the Table

In this exercise, you will narrow the first column to accommodate the headings in your résumé. When you enter background information in the second column, you will see that the rows grow taller as you type. When you reach the end of the table, you will need to add rows. Not a problem. When the insertion point is in the last cell, you simply tap Tab to generate a new row.

1. Follow these steps to decrease the width of the first column:

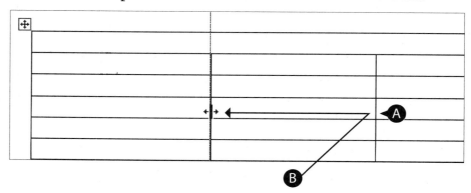

Ⓐ Position the mouse pointer on the vertical line between the columns so it changes to a double-headed arrow (resize pointer) with the arrows pointing left and right.

Ⓑ Hold down the mouse button and drag the resize pointer to the left until the first column is approximately 1.5 inches wide. (Don't worry about being exact. You can always resize later.)

Now you'll enter the contact information in the first row.

2. Click in the first row so the insertion point appears.

3. Type **Victor Gomez** and tap Enter.

4. Type the rest of the contact information as shown, tapping Enter at the end of each line except the last line.

If your Show/Hide button is still turned on, you will see the paragraph symbols at the end of each line when you tap Enter. Feel free to turn Show/Hide on and off as you prefer.

Victor Gomez
123 Cherry Blossom Lane
Windy Hills, CA 94941
415-555-1212
victor@yahoo.com

5. Tap [Tab] to move to the first cell of the second row.

   When you tap [Tab] following Victor's email address, it becomes blue and underlined. This is an email link. If Victor were to email his résumé, the recipient could click the link to open a new email with Victor's email address in the To line.

   Now you will skip a row to add white space between the contact information in the first row and the first line of the résumé.

6. Tap [Tab] two more times to move the insertion point to the first cell in the third row, and then type **Objective**.

7. Tap [Tab] to move to the next cell and type the following: **A challenging career where I can use my sales and communications skills**

   The information should fit on one line and not wrap. If it did wrap, don't worry. You can adjust the columns later. Again, you will leave a blank row so there's white space between the text entries to aid in readability.

8. Tap [Tab] three times to leave a blank row and move to the first cell of the fifth row.

9. Type **Qualifications** and tap [Tab] to move to the second cell of the fifth row.

Add Bullets in the Table

Now you will add bullets to the information in the second column to make it easy for the recipient to locate the important points about Victor's background. You apply bullets in a table the same way you do in the rest of a Word document.

10. Choose **Home→Paragraph→Bullets** [≣] to insert a bullet in the cell.

11. Type **Proven ability to close sales** and tap [Enter].

    Tapping [Enter] generates the next bullet.

12. Type **Superb communications and presentation skills** and tap [Enter] to generate the next bullet.

13. Type **Ability to quickly gain client rapport** but don't tap [Enter].

    You are now ready to move down two rows in the table.

14. Tap [Tab] three times and type **Education**.

15. Tap [Tab] again then choose **Home→Paragraph→Bullets** [≣].

16. Type the information shown. Don't tap [Enter] after the third item.

> - B.S. Sales and Marketing, Windy Hills University, 2016
> - B.S. Communications, Windy Hills University, 2016
> - 3.9 Grade Point Average

Add a Row to the End of the Table

17. Tap `Tab` to add a new row to the table.

When you use `Tab` to add a row, the new row takes on the formatting of the previous row. Which in this case means a bullet appears in the second cell. But this row should be completely blank with no bullets, so you'll change that.

18. Tap `Tab` to move to the second cell of the row.

19. Choose **Home→Paragraph→Bullets** to turn off bullets in the new row.

20. Tap `Tab` to add another new row.

21. Type the rest of the information as shown. Remember to tap `Enter` to generate a new bullet; tap `Tab` to move from cell to cell and to add a new row at the end of the table. Turn bullets on and off as needed. Adjust the column widths to your satisfaction.

Remember, click `Backspace` or `Delete` or use Undo if you make a mistake.

Computer Skills	• Microsoft Word, Excel, PowerPoint, and Access • Contact Management Software
Work Experience	• Waiter, family restaurant, summers during high school • Customer Support Assistant, Windy Hills Community Hospital, summers and weekends during college
Student Government	• Student Body President, Senior Year • Class President, Junior Year • Student Council, Membership Coordinator, Sophomore Year

Remember, you can resize columns if necessary.

22. Click the **Save** button on the Quick Access toolbar in the upper-left corner of the Word window.

Removing Table Borders

The table borders make it easy to see where you are working as you add text to a table; however, a résumé might look sleeker without borders. You'll use the Borders button in the Borders group of the Design tab to remove the table borders.

You click the menu button on the Borders button to open the menu. Clicking directly on the button face (top half of the button) applies the border style that was last chosen from the menu.

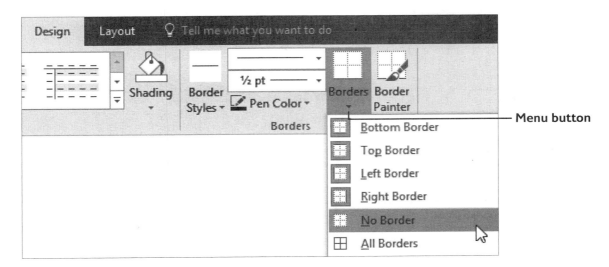

 HANDS-ON 2.9 Remove Table Borders and Print Your Résumé

In this exercise, you will remove the borders from the table. Then you will print the résumé.

1. Position the mouse pointer in the margin to the left of the first row of the table.

2. Press and hold the mouse button and drag down in the margin to the last row of the table.
   This selects the entire table.

3. Release the mouse button.

4. Choose **Table Tools→Design→Borders→Borders** menu button ▾ to display the border choices.

5. Choose **No Border** from the menu.
   You may see dotted gridlines, which are visible by default, but they are not the same as borders. They will not print. Now you will print your résumé.

6. Choose **File→Print**.

7. Click the **Print** button in the Backstage view center panel.

8. Save and close your file.

Creating an Envelope

Word makes creating envelopes easy. You type the recipient's address and your return address in the Envelopes and Labels dialog box. If you attach the envelope to a letter with a recipient address, Word will use the recipient address to automatically fill in the delivery address.

The recipient's address goes in the Delivery Address field.

The return address goes here.

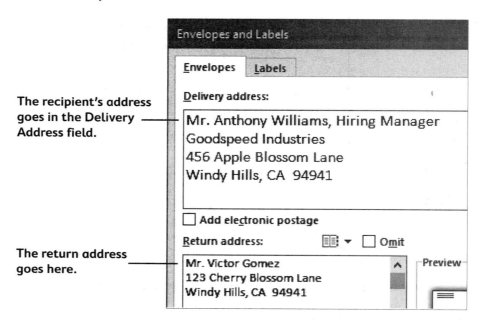

HANDS-ON 2.10 Type an Envelope

In this exercise, you will type an envelope so Victor can send his résumé to the hiring manager at Goodspeed Industries. You will attach an envelope to your cover letter.

1. Choose **File→Open** and navigate to your file storage location.

2. Open your **Cover Letter** file.

3. Choose **Mailings→Create→Envelopes** ⬚.
   The Envelopes and Labels dialog box appears. Word recognized the recipient address as the delivery address and automatically filled it in for you.

4. If an address appears in the Return Address box, click in the box and tap [Delete] or [Backspace] to remove it.

5. If a checkmark appears in the Omit checkbox above the Return Address box, click the **checkbox** to remove it.

6. Click in the **Return Address** field and type this address:

   `Mr. Victor Gomez`
   `123 Cherry Blossom Lane`
   `Windy Hills, CA 94941`

7. Click the **Add to Document** button at the bottom of the dialog box.

8. Click **No** when prompted to save the return address.

   Notice that the envelope is attached to the cover letter.

   If you are not familiar with printing envelopes, you should consult your printer manual. The steps for loading and printing envelopes can vary from printer to printer.

9. Make sure the insertion point is in the envelope and choose **File→Print**.

   You would choose Print Current Page *from the button shown here. This would prevent the cover letter from printing again.*

10. In this example, you will bypass printing the envelope.

11. Click the **Save** command in the panel on the left and then close the file.

Self-Assessment

Check your knowledge of this chapter's key concepts and skills by completing the Self-Assessment.

Page number

1. Word Wrap keeps certain lines short, such as a greeting line in a letter.   **true false** _____

2. You made a change to a letter after saving and naming it. To save the new change, you must choose Save As.   **true false** _____

3. You can use [Enter] to create blank lines in a document, such as the blank lines following the date in a letter.   **true false** _____

4. You use the Show/Hide [¶] button to display and hide nonprinting characters.   **true false** _____

5. AutoComplete recognizes certain words, such as names of months and days of the week.   **true false** _____

6. You should NOT use [Enter] to end lines *within* a paragraph.   **true false** _____

7. The default (preassigned) line spacing in Word 2016 is _____.

   A. 1.0

   B. 1.15

   C. 1.08

   D. 2.0

   Page number: _____

8. Which of these is a characteristic of Word tables?

   A. They are made up of cells.

   B. They use Word Wrap to navigate between rows.

   C. You cannot adjust column widths.

   D. Live Preview does not work with them.

   Page number: _____

9. You can add a row at the end of a table by tapping _____.

   A. [Tab]

   B. [Enter]

   C. [Ctrl]

   D. [Backspace]

   Page number: _____

10. Which keystroke creates a nonprinting character?

    A. [Enter]

    B. [Page Up]

    C. [Delete]

    D. [Shift]

    Page number: _____

Skill Builders

SKILL BUILDER 2.1 **Write a Letter to a Friend**

In this exercise, you will conduct online research to find hints for writing a great résumé. Then you will send a letter to a friend who is looking for a job, sharing the information you've discovered. Since this is not a formal business letter, you will use Word's default 1.08 line spacing.

1. Start a new document based on the **Blank Document** template.

2. Open your web browser and navigate to Google by typing **google.com** (or choose the search engine you prefer.)

3. Click the **Search** box, type **hints for good resumes**, and tap Enter .

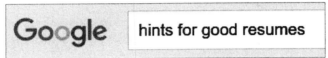

Ask your instructor for assistance if you are not familiar with web searches.

4. Make a note of the four hints you think are the most important.

5. Return to Word and use these guidelines to type the text of the letter that follows:

    -   Tap Enter six times so the letter will be centered vertically (with equal space above and below) on the page.

    -   Use AutoComplete to enter today's date.

    -   Let Word Wrap do its thing. Don't be concerned if your line widths don't match the illustration.

    -   Enter the information you found online after the bullets and in place of the word *Hint*.

- Use the paragraph symbols shown in the letter as a guide for when to tap Enter .

- Use Backspace , Delete , or Undo ↶ if you make a mistake.

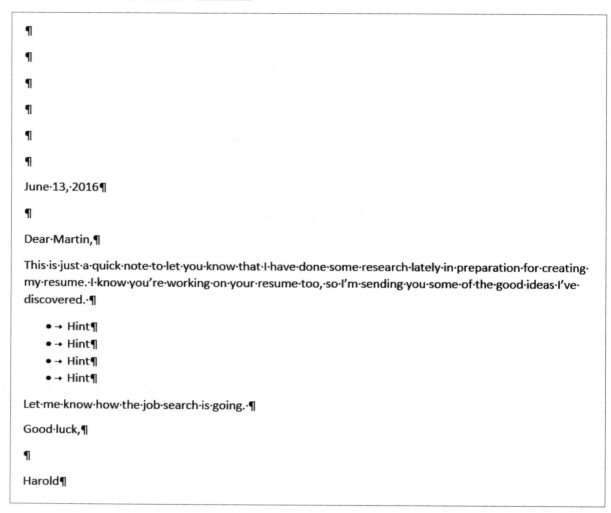

¶

¶

¶

¶

¶

¶

June·13,·2016¶

¶

Dear·Martin,¶

This·is·just·a·quick·note·to·let·you·know·that·I·have·done·some·research·lately·in·preparation·for·creating·my·resume.·I·know·you're·working·on·your·resume·too,·so·I'm·sending·you·some·of·the·good·ideas·I've·discovered.·¶

   •→ Hint¶
   •→ Hint¶
   •→ Hint¶
   •→ Hint¶

Let·me·know·how·the·job·search·is·going.·¶

Good·luck,¶

¶

Harold¶

6. Save your letter in your file storage location as **sb-Letter to Martin**.

- -

SKILL BUILDER 2.2 Create an Envelope

In this exercise, you will create an envelope and attach it to the letter you just typed.

1. Choose **Mailings→Create→Envelopes** ⬚.

2. If necessary, delete any address information in the Delivery Address box by tapping Delete or Backspace .

3. Type this address in the Delivery Address area:

   `Mr. Martin Nguyen`
   `654 Willow Lane`
   `Wheeling, WV 26003`

4. If necessary, delete any information in the Return Address box.

5. If there's a checkmark in the Omit box above Return Address, click the **checkbox** to remove the checkmark.

6. Type this address in the Return Address area:

   `Harold Frost`
   `789 Elm Street`
   `Martins Ferry, OH 43935`

7. Click the **Add to Document** button.

8. Click **No** when prompted to save the return address.

9. Save and close your file.

· ·

SKILL BUILDER 2.3 Manage Your Mysteries with a Table

In this exercise, you will keep track of your mystery novels that are on loan to your friends. You have quite a large collection, and keeping track of who has borrowed a book is becoming a mystery to you. You have decided to use Word's Table feature to keep track of your books.

1. Start a new document based on the **Blank Document** template.

2. Choose **Insert→Tables→Table** ▦.
   The table grid appears.

3. Position the mouse pointer in the upper-left corner of the grid and then hold down the mouse button and drag to the right to select four columns. Keep the mouse button down.

4. Drag the mouse pointer down to the sixth row; release the mouse button.
   A 4x6 table is created. Now you will enter the column headings.

5. Make sure the insertion point is in the first cell of the first row and type:
   `On Loan To`

6. Tap Tab to position the insertion point in the second cell of the first row and type: `Title`

7. Tap [Tab] again and type: **Author**

8. Tap [Tab] one more time and type: **Main Character**

9. Tap [Tab] to move the insertion point to the first cell of the second row and type: **Brady**

10. Enter the information shown, starting with the second cell in the second row:

On Loan To	Title	Author	Main Character
Brady	Caribbean Mystery	Christie, Agatha	Miss Marple
Opal	The Last Precinct	Cornwell, Patricia	Dr. Kay Scarpetta
Devon	In the Last Analysis	Cross, Amanda	Kate Fensler
Stella	One for the Money	Evanovich, Janet	Stephanie Plum
Matt	Playing for the Ashes	George, Elizabeth	Thomas Lynley

Your friend Lucy just came by to borrow one of your mysteries. Now you'll need to add a row to the bottom of the table.

11. Make sure the insertion point is in the last cell of the table.

12. Tap [Tab] to add a new row to the bottom of the table.

13. Type the new row as shown:

Lucy	B is for Burglar	Grafton, Sue	Kinsey Millhone

14. Save the file in your file storage location as **sb-Mysteries on Loan** and then close it.

15. Exit Word.

Editing the Business Etiquette Column

Editing documents in Word is an easy task, and Word provides many automatic features to assist you. The Undo feature lets you back out of a mistake instead of trying to fix it. The Spelling & Grammar checker keeps an eye out as you type and alerts you to possible errors. And Word will find terms you are looking for and even replace them automatically if you like. In this chapter, you will learn useful techniques for editing your Word documents.

LEARNING OBJECTIVES

- Use a variety of techniques for selecting text
- Edit documents and use Undo, Redo, and AutoCorrect
- Use the Spelling & Grammar checker
- Move and copy text
- Automatically find and replace text in a document

Project: Using the Spelling & Grammar Checker and the Find Feature

Tyrone Williams writes a monthly business etiquette column for the *Windy Hills University Review* so graduating students can start thinking about the human relations skills that are so important in the corporate environment. Tyrone finds Word's Spelling & Grammar checker to be a great aid in helping him write an error-free column. The checker constantly monitors spelling, allowing him to correct errors as he types.

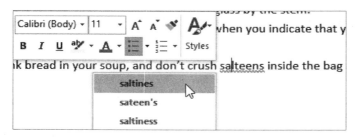

Word's Find feature allows Tyrone to move around quickly in his business etiquette column.

There are three ways to browse through a document.

Enter the text to find here.

The search results terms are highlighted in the document.

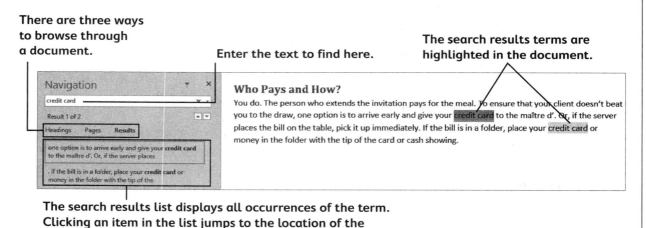

The search results list displays all occurrences of the term. Clicking an item in the list jumps to the location of the item in the document.

Selecting Text

In Word, you select (highlight) text in order to do something to it. For example, you select text before moving or copying it. You also select text when you want to replace or format it.

You work with two different areas of the screen when selecting text:

- The selection bar (in the left margin of a document)
- The typing area (between the margins)

When you select text, the Mini toolbar appears. You can ignore it in this chapter. The Mini toolbar contains commands for formatting text, which you will learn more about later in this course.

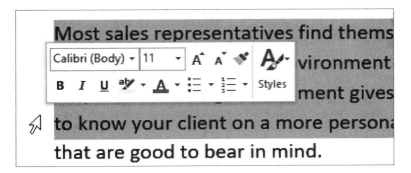

Selection Bar

The selection bar is in the left margin of a document. When the mouse pointer is in the selection bar, it looks like a white, right-tilting arrow.

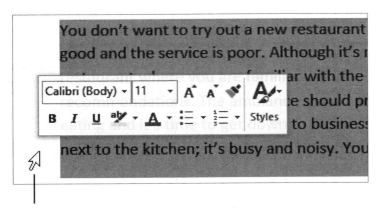

The mouse pointer is in the selection bar.

Typing Area

The mouse pointer looks like an I-beam $\boxed{\text{I}}$ when you select text in the typing area, which is the area between the margins.

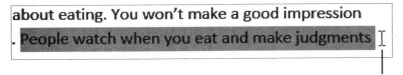

The mouse pointer is in the typing area.

Selection Techniques

A primary method for selecting text is to click and drag the mouse pointer. In addition, Word provides mouse and keyboard shortcuts for selecting text.

SELECTING TEXT		
Item to Be Selected	**Mouse Procedure**	**Keyboard Procedure**
One word	Double-click the word.	Click at the beginning of the word and press Shift+Ctrl while tapping →.
Continuous block of text	Press the left mouse button while dragging the mouse pointer over the desired text.	Click at the beginning of the text and tap Shift while tapping an arrow key. Or, click at the beginning of the text, tap Shift, and click at the end of the text.
A line	Place the mouse pointer in the selection bar and click.	Press Shift+End to select from the insertion point to the end of the line. Press Shift+Home to select from the insertion point to the beginning of the line.
A sentence	Hold down Ctrl and click the mouse pointer in the sentence.	
One paragraph	Triple-click anywhere in the paragraph or position the mouse pointer in the selection bar and double-click.	
Multiple paragraphs	Drag the I-beam over the desired paragraphs or position the mouse pointer in the selection bar and drag to select.	
Entire document	Triple-click in the selection bar or tap Ctrl and click in the selection bar.	Press Ctrl+A.
Nonadjacent areas	Select the first block of text and then tap Ctrl while dragging over additional blocks of text.	

🖰 HANDS-ON 3.1 Select Text

In this exercise, you will select text from the selection bar and the typing area using both mouse and keyboard techniques. You'll start with the selection bar.

1. Start Word.

2. Click the **Open Other Documents** link at the bottom of the left side of the Start screen.

3. Navigate to your **Chapter 03** folder and click the **Professional Polish** file to select it.

4. Click the **Open** button in the bottom-right corner of the dialog box.

Select Text from the Selection Bar

5. Place the mouse pointer in the selection bar at the left edge of the screen just to the left of the first line of the first paragraph.

    The mouse pointer changes to a right-tilting arrow.

    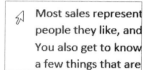

6. Click once to select the first line.

    Most sales representatives find themselves dining with their clients from time to time. People buy from people they like, and the dining environment gives your client an opportunity to get to know you better. You also get to know your client on a more personal level. To ensure a successful dining event, there are

    The Mini toolbar appears when you select text. Ignore it for now; it will fade away.

7. Double-click in the **selection bar** to select the entire paragraph.

    Most sales representatives find themselves dining with their clients from time to time. People buy from people they like, and the dining environment gives your client an opportunity to get to know you better. You also get to know your client on a more personal level. To ensure a successful dining event, there are a few things that are good to bear in mind.

8. Triple-click in the **selection bar** to select the entire document.

    If you find triple-clicking difficult, press ⌈Ctrl⌉+⌈A⌉ to select the entire document.

9. Position the mouse pointer in the typing area and click once to deselect (remove the highlighting).

    Remember, clicking once in the selection bar selects an entire line. To remove all highlighting, you must click in the typing area.

Select Text in the Typing Area

10. Position the mouse pointer over the word *Most* at the beginning of the first line of the first paragraph.

11. Double-click to select the word.

> Most sales representatives
> people they like, and the di
> You also get to know your c
> a few things that are good t

12. Click once in the **typing area** to deselect the text.

13. Position the mouse pointer somewhere in the first sentence; hold Ctrl and click.

This selects the entire sentence.

> Most sales representatives find themselves dining with their clients from time to time. People buy from people they like, and the dining environment gives your client an opportunity to get to know you better.

14. Click once in the **typing area** to deselect the highlighted text.

Select Text with the Keyboard

15. Position the insertion point at the beginning of the first line of the first paragraph.

16. Press Shift and then click at the end of the paragraph.

This selects everything from the insertion point to the Shift -and-click position.

17. Release Shift and then click once in the **typing area** to deselect the text.

18. Position the insertion point at the beginning of the first paragraph again.

19. Press Ctrl + Shift and then tap → several times to select one word at a time.

20. Release Ctrl + Shift and then tap any **arrow key** to deselect the text.

Always leave your document open unless directed otherwise.

· ·

Editing Techniques

You know that the Delete and Backspace keys delete one character at a time. Word has several other ways you can edit text, including adding, deleting, and replacing selected blocks of text. Word will even help you edit with its AutoCorrect feature.

Add, Delete, and Replace Text

To add text to an existing document, simply position the insertion point where you want the new text to appear and begin typing. Word will make room for the new text as you type, while Word Wrap keeps the paragraph nicely organized.

You can delete a block of text all at once by selecting the text and tapping $\boxed{\text{Delete}}$. Word Wrap then closes up the gap and rewraps the text.

To replace existing text, select the text to replace and type the new text in its place. It doesn't matter if the selected text block is larger or smaller than the text replacing it. The surrounding text expands or collapses to accommodate the new text.

QUICK REFERENCE: Editing Text

Task	Procedure
Add text	Position the insertion point where you want the new text to appear and begin typing.
Delete text	Position the insertion point where you want to delete text and then tap $\boxed{\text{Backspace}}$ (erase to the left) or $\boxed{\text{Delete}}$ (erase to the right). Or, select a block of text and tap $\boxed{\text{Delete}}$.
Replace text	Select the text to be replaced and then type the new text in its place.

AutoCorrect

Word has a wonderful feature called AutoCorrect that automatically corrects misspelled words and typos for you as you type. For example, if you type *aboutthe*, AutoCorrect changes it to *about the*. It corrects other errors, too, such as incorrect capitalization if you accidentally tap $\boxed{\text{Caps Lock}}$ while typing.

HANDS-ON 3.2 Use AutoCorrect and Edit Text

In this exercise, you will work with AutoCorrect and add, delete, and replace text. You will begin by adding a bullet point at the end of page 2. You will purposely make mistakes so you can watch Word automatically correct them for you.

1. Scroll down to page 2 and position the insertion point at the end of the last bulleted item.

2. Tap $\boxed{\text{Enter}}$ to generate a new bullet.

3. Type **Turn offf** and tap $\boxed{\text{Spacebar}}$.
    Word corrects the word off.

4. Type **teh**, tap Spacebar , and watch Word change it to *the*.

5. Finish typing the bulleted item as shown:

```
Turn off the cell phone. You insult your guests when
you indicate that your phone call is more important
than they are.
```

6. Press Ctrl and tap Home to position the insertion point at the top of the document.

7. Position the insertion point at the beginning of the second sentence in the first paragraph.

Most sales representatives find themselves dining with their clients from time to time. People buy from people they like, and the dining environment gives your client an opportunity to get to know you better.

8. Type this sentence:

```
Sharing a meal provides a more relaxed environment than
the typical conference room.
```

9. Tap Spacebar .

Notice how Word makes space for the new text and how Word Wrap keeps things in order.

10. Follow these steps to select and delete text in the first paragraph:

Most sales representatives find themselves dining with their clients from time to time. Sharing a meal provides a more relaxed environment than the typic**B**conference**C**om. People buy from people they like, and the dining environment gives your cl**A**an opportunity to get to know you better. You also get to know your client on a more personal level. To ensure a successful dining event, there are a few things that are good to bear in mind.

A Position the I-beam to the left of *an*.

B Press the mouse button and drag right through the space following *opportunity*. Release the mouse button.

C Tap Delete

The insertion point should appear to the left of to.

than the typical conference
your client to get to know y
ure a successful dining even

11. Type **a chance** and tap Spacebar in place of the deleted words.

Replace Selected Text

12. Position the mouse pointer over the word *perceive* in the first line of the second paragraph; double-click to select the word.

> Why? You don't want people to perceive that you
> the business lunch or dinner is all about business,

13. Type: **think**

The word you just typed replaced the selected word.

14. Save your document.

. . . .

Spelling & Grammar Checker

Word helps you with your editing tasks. If you make a typo and AutoCorrect isn't sure how to fix it, the Spelling & Grammar checker comes to the rescue. It monitors your spelling as you type and underlines words it suspects are misspelled with a squiggly red line. Right-clicking the underlined word displays a pop-up menu with suggestions of possible correct spellings. You only need to choose the correct spelling from the menu.

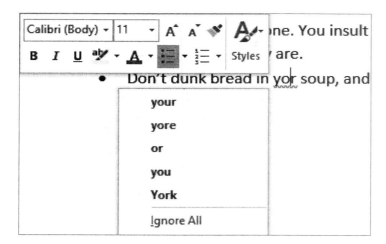

Sometimes the Spelling & Grammar checker marks a word as a possible misspelling when it's correct. Some proper names fall into that category, although the checker has many common proper names in its dictionary and does not mark them. If Word marks a term incorrectly, you can ignore the underlining (it won't print), choose Ignore All, or choose Add to Dictionary from the pop-up menu.

Grammar and Context Checking

Word checks for possible grammatical and contextual errors and marks them with a squiggly blue underline. As you'll find with the Spelling checker, you can ignore the underline, right-click the term and choose a replacement, or choose Ignore.

Undo and Redo

The Undo and Redo buttons appear on the Quick Access toolbar. You've likely had a little experience with Undo by now. If you undo something and then change your mind, that's where Redo comes in. You can redo what you undid!

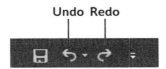

How Undo Helps You

Clicking Undo reverses your last action. If you click Undo again, the next-to-last action is reversed, and then the next-to-last from that, and so forth. Essentially, you are backing your way out of the problem. If you go too far or change your mind, just use Redo.

You can get out of most any catastrophe if you click Undo enough times. If you get into a mess, don't try to fix it; just undo it!

What Undo Can and Cannot Undo

Undo works for things you do that make modifications to a document: inserting text, editing text, formatting text, and so on. Undo cannot reverse actions like saving a document or selecting text. Once you close a document, it's too late to undo. If you want to make changes when you open the document again, you have to use editing techniques instead of the Undo feature.

HANDS-ON 3.3 Proof and Use Undo/Redo

In this exercise, you will purposely make some typos so you can see the Spelling & Grammar checker in action. You will replace a word, undo the replacement, and then redo the action.

1. Press Ctrl + End to move the insertion point to the end of the document.

2. Make sure the insertion point is at the end of the last bullet point and then tap Enter to generate the next bullet.

3. Type this sentence, taking care to purposely misspell *your* and *saltines*:

   `Don't dunk bread in yor soup, and don't crush salteens`
   `inside the bag and dump them in your soup.`

   Notice the squiggly red lines under yor *and* salteens, *indicating possible spelling errors.*

4. Place the mouse pointer over *yor* and click the right mouse button to display the pop-up menu.

5. Choose the correct spelling of *your* from the menu.

6. Right-click **salteens** and choose **saltines** from the pop-up menu.
   Now you'll use Undo and Redo.

7. Press Ctrl + Home to return to the top of the document.

8. Double-click **representatives** in the first line of the first paragraph to select it.

   > Most sales representatives find themselves provides a more relaxed environment than

9. Type **people** to replace the selected word.
   Hmmm, maybe representatives *was better.*

10. Click **Undo** ↩ on the Quick Access toolbar as many times as necessary to return to the original word.
    Now you decide you prefer people.

11. Click **Redo** ↪ on the Quick Access toolbar as many times as necessary to return to *people*.

12. Save your document.

Moving and Copying Text

When you move text, you remove it from its original position and place it in a new location. When you copy text, the original text remains intact and a copy is placed in the new location—it's in both places. You can use the Cut, Copy, and Paste buttons in the Clipboard group on the Home tab to move and copy text.

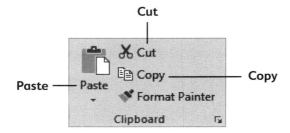

There are also handy keyboard shortcuts you can use to cut, copy, and paste.

QUICK REFERENCE: Moving and Copying Text

Task	Procedure (Ribbon)	Procedure (Keyboard)
Move text	■ Select the desired text and then choose Home→Clipboard→Cut. ■ Click at the destination and then choose Home→Clipboard→Paste.	■ Select the desired text and then press ⌈Ctrl⌉+⌈X⌉ to cut. ■ Click at the destination and then press ⌈Ctrl⌉+⌈V⌉ to paste.
Copy text	■ Select the desired text and then choose Home→Clipboard→Copy. ■ Click at the destination and then choose Home→Clipboard→Paste.	■ Select the desired text and then press ⌈Ctrl⌉+⌈C⌉ to copy. ■ Click at the destination and then press ⌈Ctrl⌉+⌈V⌉ to paste.

 HANDS-ON 3.4 Move and Copy Text

In this exercise, you will move and copy text using both Ribbon and keyboard techniques. You'll start by moving the *Consider Various Tastes* paragraph above the *Eat Before Dinner* paragraph.

1. Position the mouse pointer in the selection bar to the left of the *Consider Various Tastes* heading and then press the mouse button and drag down through the last line of the paragraph.

Consider Various Tastes
Choose a restaurant that offers variety. Remember, your clients could have strict eating guidelines. Some will look for a low-calorie offering on the menu. Others may prefer vegetarian dining, and religious differences can also determine what people will eat.

2. Choose **Home→Clipboard→Cut** ✂.

3. Position the insertion point to the left of the *Eat Before Dinner* heading.

4. Choose **Home→Clipboard→Paste** 📋.

Eat Before Dinner
Why? You don't want people to

Now you'll use keystrokes to move the Choose a Familiar Restaurant *paragraph above the* Eat Before Dinner *paragraph.*

5. Position the mouse pointer in the **selection bar** to the left of the *Choose a Familiar Restaurant* heading.

6. Click the mouse button and drag down through the last line of the paragraph.

7. Press Ctrl+X to cut the paragraph.

8. Position the insertion point to the left of the *Eat Before Dinner* heading.

9. Press Ctrl+V to paste the paragraph in the new location.

Copy Text with the Mouse and the Keyboard

10. Scroll to the end of page 2 and place the insertion point at the end of the last bullet point.

11. Tap Enter three times to set off an area where you will copy information to.

12. Click and drag in the **selection bar** to select the first bullet point.

13. Choose **Home→Clipboard→Copy** 📋.

14. Position the insertion point at the bottom of the page.

15. Choose **Home→Clipboard→Paste** 📋.

    That information now appears in two places on the page.

16. Position the mouse pointer in the selection bar to the left of the second bullet point and click to select the line.

17. Press Ctrl+C to copy the information.

18. Position the insertion point at the bottom of the page.

19. Press Ctrl+V to create a copy of the information.

20. Press Ctrl+Home to move back to the top of the document.

21. Save your document.

. . . .

Finding and Replacing Text

What do you do when you need to locate a specific word or phrase in a long document? Let Word locate it for you with the Find feature! There is also a slightly more advanced Find and Replace feature that helps you find existing text and automatically replace it with new text. As an example, this is a handy tool if you accidentally misspell a

proper noun throughout a document. The Find and Replace commands appear in the Editing group at the right end of the Home tab.

Find with the Navigation Pane

The Find command opens the Navigation pane on the left side of the screen. When you search for a term, the items found conveniently appear in the results list, giving you an overview of everywhere the term appears. Clicking an item in the search results list causes Word to jump to that location in the document. The search terms are also highlighted in the document.

There are three ways to browse through a document.

Enter the text to find here.

The search results terms are highlighted in the document.

The search results list displays all occurrences of the term. Clicking an item in the list jumps to the location of the item in the document.

The Find and Replace Dialog Box

The Replace option in the Editing group on the Home tab displays the Find and Replace dialog box, where you can enter the text you want to find and the replacement text.

You type the term you want to find here.

You type the term you want to replace it with here.

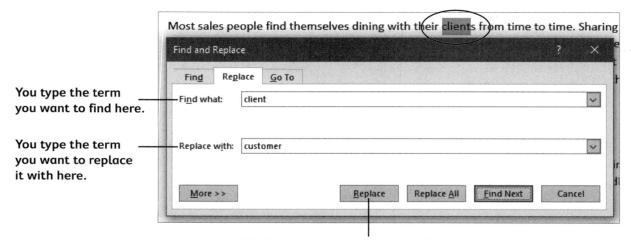

Clicking the Replace button makes the replacement.

Although the search term is *client*, notice in the previous figure that Word found the plural form *clients*. That's because the word *client* is embedded in the word *clients*. Word will make the replacement, maintaining the plural form when appropriate.

QUICK REFERENCE: Finding and Replacing Text

Task	Procedure
Find text	■ Choose Home→Editing→Find and then type the search term in the search box.
	■ Click an item in the search results list to scroll the document to that occurrence of the term.
Replace text	■ Choose Home→Editing→Replace and then type the search term in the Find What box.
	■ Type the replacement term in the Replace With box and then click Find Next.
	■ Click Replace to replace the first instance of the text or click Find Next to skip to the next occurrence of the search term. Or, click Replace All to make all replacements at once.

Warning! Be confident about the changes that will occur when you use Replace All. If you are unsure, use Replace to monitor each replacement.

⌖ HANDS-ON 3.5 Use Find and Find and Replace

In this exercise, you will use Find to locate the term credit cards. Then you'll use Find and Replace to locate the word client and replace it with customer.

1. If necessary, make sure the insertion point is at the top of the document.

2. Choose **Home→Editing→Find** 🔍 to open the Navigation pane.

Tip! Click directly on the button face of the Find button. Clicking the menu button (▼) on the right side of the Find button opens a menu that you won't use in this chapter.

3. Type **credit card** in the box at the top of the Navigation pane.

Both occurrences of the term appear in the search results list of the Navigation pane and both terms are highlighted in the document.

4. Click **Close** ☒ in the upper-right corner of the Navigation pane to close it.

   Now you will find the word client *and replace it with* customer.

5. Position the insertion point at the top of the document.

6. Choose **Home→Editing→Replace** 🔤.

   The Find and Replace dialog box opens. Word remembers the last term you searched for and places it in the Find What field. You will just ignore it and type the new term you are searching for over the top of the old search term.

7. Follow these steps to begin replacing *client* with *customer*:

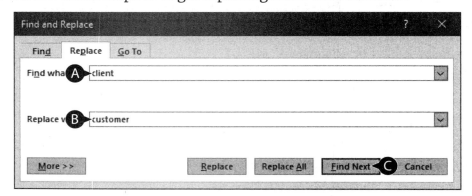

   Ⓐ Type **client** in the Find What box.

   Ⓑ Type **customer** in the Replace With box.

   Ⓒ Click **Find Next**.

   Word highlights the first occurrence of the word. You may have to move the Find and Replace dialog box to see the highlighted word. If so, place your mouse pointer on the title bar of the top of the dialog box, press the mouse button, and drag the dialog box to a new location.

8. Click the **Replace** button at the bottom of the dialog box.

   Notice that Word made customer *plural like* clients, *which it is replacing. Word also highlights the next occurrence of the word.*

9. Click the **Replace** button again.

10. Continue clicking **Replace** as each term is highlighted until you see a message indicting that Word has finished searching the document.

11. Click **OK** to close the message.

12. Click the **Close** button in the Find and Replace dialog box.

13. Save and close your document.

Self-Assessment

Check your knowledge of this chapter's key concepts and skills by completing the Self-Assessment.

Page number

1. You select text in order to do something with it, such as move or copy it.　　**true　false**　_____

2. When you use the Undo feature, you are essentially backing your way out of a problem.　　**true　false**　_____

3. When you copy text, the original text remains intact and a copy is placed in the new location.　　**true　false**　_____

4. When you delete a block of text within a paragraph, you must manually rewrap the lines using Enter.　　**true　false**　_____

5. When you use the Replace feature, Word always knows the correct replacements to make when you use the Replace All button.　　**true　false**　_____

6. The Find feature uses the Navigation pane to help you locate terms in your documents.　　**true　false**　_____

7. The Spelling & Grammar checker _____.

   A. underlines misspelled words with a squiggly green line

   B. corrects all misspelled proper names

   C. is a subset of the AutoCorrect feature

   D. underlines misspelled words with a squiggly red line

   Page number: _____

8. To select a single word with the mouse, _____.

   A. triple-click it

   B. press Ctrl and click it

   C. double-click it

   D. position the mouse pointer in the selection bar and drag up or down

   Page number: _____

9. The AutoCorrect feature _____.

   A. automatically inserts the date

   B. is located on the Quick Access toolbar

   C. corrects line spacing

   D. automatically corrects misspelled words and typos

   Page number: _____

10. Undo works for _____.

    A. things you do that make modifications to a document

    B. printing

    C. saving a document

    D. selecting text

    Page number: _____

Skill Builders

SKILL BUILDER 3.1 **Select Text and Use Undo and Redo**

In this exercise, you will select text using both the mouse and the keyboard. You will also use the Undo and Redo features.

1. Open **sb-Options** from your **Chapter 03** folder.

Select Text with the Mouse

2. Place the mouse pointer in the selection bar to the left of the first main paragraph and then double-click to select the entire paragraph.

3. Place the mouse pointer in the typing area and click once to deselect the text.

4. Select the paragraph again, but this time click and drag in the **selection bar** to select it.

5. Click in the **typing area** to deselect.

6. Double-click the word *option* in the first sentence of the first paragraph to select it.

7. Click in the **typing area** to deselect.

Select Text with the Keyboard

8. Position the insertion point at the beginning of the *Interest Rate Options* paragraph.

9. Press Shift and then click at the end of the paragraph to select the entire paragraph.

10. Release Shift .

11. Tap any **arrow key** on the keyboard to deselect.

12. Click at the beginning of the *Interest Rate Options* paragraph.

13. Press Shift + End to select the entire line.

14. Tap any **arrow key** to deselect.

Use Undo and Redo

15. Hold down Ctrl and click the first sentence of the *Equity Options* paragraph to select the entire sentence.

16. Tap Delete .

17. Click **Undo** ↶ on the Quick Access toolbar to undo the deletion.

18. Click **Redo** ↪ on the Quick Access toolbar to delete the sentence again.

19. Click **Undo** ↩ to undelete the sentence again.

20. Save your file and keep it open for the next exercise.

··

SKILL BUILDER 3.2 Move and Copy Text

In this exercise, you will move and copy text. To begin, you will move the Equity Options paragraph above the Interest Rate Options paragraph.

1. Select the *Equity Options* heading and its following paragraph.

2. Choose **Home→Clipboard→Cut** ✂.

3. Position the insertion point in front of the *Interest Rate Options* heading.

4. Choose **Home→Clipboard→Paste** 📋 to move the text to the new location.

5. Scroll down to page 2.
   Now you will copy text.

6. Select the *Interest Rate Swap* heading and its following paragraph.

7. Choose **Home→Clipboard→Copy** 🗐.

8. Press ⌈Ctrl⌉+⌈End⌉ to place the insertion point at the end of the document.

9. Choose **Home→Clipboard→Paste** 📋 to place a copy of the paragraph at the end of the document.

10. Scroll to the top of the page and select the *Interest Rate Swap* heading and its following paragraph again.

11. Tap ⌈Delete⌉ to remove the original paragraph.

12. Save and close the file.

··

SKILL BUILDER 3.3 Add, Delete, and Replace Text

In this exercise, you will open a document and make editing changes to it. You will add, delete, and replace text.

1. Open **sb-Ripe Fruit** from your **Chapter 03** folder.
   Locate the paragraph that begins with Apples, bananas, avocados.... *This is where you will make the first editing changes.*

2. Position the insertion point between the word *tomatoes* and the comma in the first line of the paragraph.

3. Tap [Spacebar] and type this text: **(yes, tomatoes are fruits)**

4. Toward the beginning of the next line, double-click to select the word *vine* and type **plant** in its place.

> Apples, bananas, avocados will ripen off the vine. In fa tropical fruits will ripen off

5. Toward the end of the third line, position the insertion point just after the word *yields*, tap [Spacebar], and type this text: **(but is not mushy)**

6. In the second-to-last line of the same paragraph, position the insertion point between the word *gas* and the comma, tap [Spacebar], and type this text: **(ripening agent)**

7. In the last sentence of the paragraph, click to the left of the word *bag*, type **paper**, and tap [Spacebar].

8. In the first bullet point, double-click the word *broken* and replace it with: **split**

9. In the second bullet point, double-click the word *wrinkled* and replace it with **shriveled**.

10. In the second sentence of the fifth bullet point, position the insertion point between the word *pull* and the comma.

11. Tap [Spacebar] and type: **off**

12. In the last sentence on the page, double-click the word *usually* and tap [Delete].

13. Save and close the file.

. . . .

SKILL BUILDER 3.4 Use Find and Find and Replace

In this exercise, you will use Find to locate a term. You will also use Find and Replace to make changes to the document.

1. Open **sb-Energy Inspection** from your **Chapter 03** folder.

2. Choose **Home→Editing→Find** 🔍 to open the Navigation pane.

3. Type **esl** in the search box at the top of the Navigation pane.
   Word locates the term in the document.

4. Click **Close** ⊗ in the upper-right corner of the Navigation pane.

5. Make sure the insertion point is positioned at the top of the document.

Use Find and Replace

6. Choose **Home→Editing→Replace** ![ab-ac icon].

7. Type `offenders` in the **Find What** box and `wasters` in the **Replace With** box.

8. Click the **Find Next** button.

The word Offenders *is highlighted.*

9. Click the **Replace** button to replace *Offenders* with *Wasters*.

Word highlights the next occurrence of offenders.

10. Click the **Replace** button again.

A message appears to let you know that Word has finished searching the document.

11. Click **OK** to close the message.

12. Type `recent` in the **Find What** box and `the latest` in the **Replace With** box.

13. Click the **Find Next** button.

14. Click the **Replace** button to replace *Recent* with *The latest*.

15. When the message appears, click **OK**.

16. Click the **Close** button to close the Find and Replace dialog box.

17. Save and close the file.

....

SKILL BUILDER 3.5 Use the Spelling & Grammar Checker

You're heading up a green construction project and are looking for volunteers to participate in the project. In this exercise, you will correct errors the spelling checker found in your project file.

1. Open **sb-Green Construction** from your **Chapter 03** folder.

Notice the misspelled words, as indicated by the red squiggly underlines.

2. Right-click the word *Fluoorescent* in the sixth bullet point and select the correct spelling at the top of the pop-up menu.

3. Right-click the word *matterials* in the eighth bullet point and select the correct spelling at the top of the pop-up menu.

4. Correct the word *sustaainable* in the next bullet point.

5. Correct *Construcion* in the last line.

6. Save and close the file.

7. Exit Word.

....

Encouraging Recycling with Flyers

In this chapter, you will create a dynamic flyer in Word. Flyers provide a great way to advertise an event, product, or idea. Word has many ways to create exciting flyers, including inserting graphic images and creating stylized WordArt. You will work with character formatting and will also manipulate images to meet your needs.

LEARNING OBJECTIVES

- Apply formatting from the Ribbon and Mini toolbar
- Use Live Preview and galleries
- Change paragraph alignment
- Work with WordArt and clip art images
- Create new folders for organizing documents

📂 Project: Promoting Recycling

Hayden DeLaurentis is a student teacher at a local high school. The earth sciences students are about to begin a recycling project, and Hayden wants to create a flyer to promote interest in the project. This is an opportunity to practice character formatting and to use some of Word's fun tools, such as WordArt and clip art.

Reduce, Reuse, Recycle

- Separate your trash
- Always look for recycle bins
- Reuse shopping bags
- If it's broken, fix it
- Buy recycled products
- Take along reusable cups
- Use washable napkins

Do Your Part!

Formatting with the Ribbon

Character formatting can help you get your message across. Examples of character formats include:

- Font type
- Font style
- Font size
- Font color

Character formatting settings take effect from the insertion point forward or until you change them. If you wish to format *existing* text, you must select the text first and then format it.

Fonts

The term *font* typically refers to character design, which can vary dramatically. You can apply any font in the Font menu to change the appearance of text.

This is an example of the Calibri font.

This is an example of Comic Sans MS.

This is an example of Old English Text MT.

This is the font type that is in effect where the insertion point is positioned.

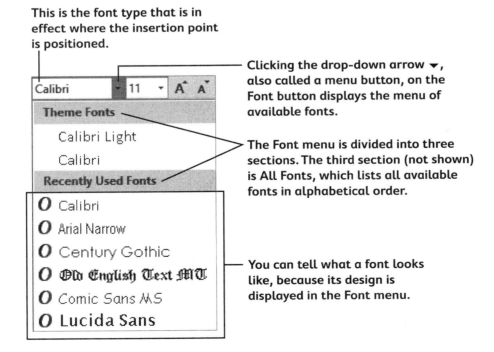

Clicking the drop-down arrow ▼, also called a menu button, on the Font button displays the menu of available fonts.

The Font menu is divided into three sections. The third section (not shown) is All Fonts, which lists all available fonts in alphabetical order.

You can tell what a font looks like, because its design is displayed in the Font menu.

The Font Group

The Font group on the Home tab provides a convenient way to format characters. The following illustration points out some frequently used font attributes.

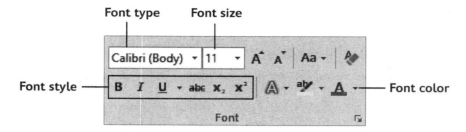

Font Size

Font size is measured in *points*, and there are 72 points in 1 inch. Frequently used sizes for typing body text (versus headings) are 10, 11, and 12 points.

Formatting with the Mini Toolbar

The Mini toolbar contains frequently used formatting commands. When you select text, the Mini toolbar appears. After a pause, this little toolbar fades away. You can make it reappear by right-clicking the selected text.

In this example, clicking the Bold B button on the Mini toolbar applies bold to the selected text.

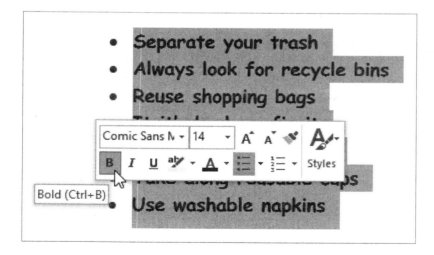

Live Preview with Galleries

Live Preview displays what a formatting change will look like without actually applying the format. In this example, selecting a block of text and then hovering the mouse pointer over a font name previews how the text will look. Clicking the font name applies the font to the selected text.

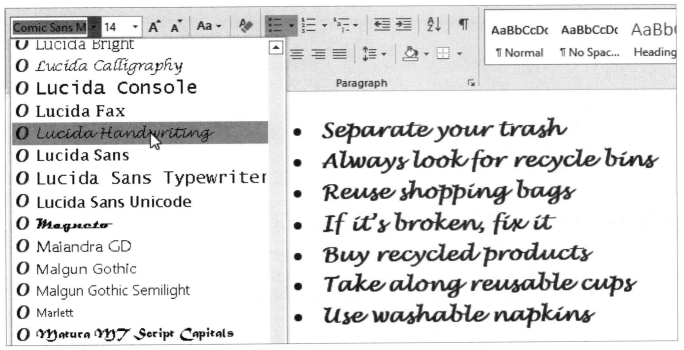

A Live Preview of the Lucida Handwriting font

HANDS-ON 4.1 Use Character Formatting

In this exercise, you will type recycling suggestions in your flyer. Then you will format characters using the Home tab's Font group and the Mini toolbar.

1. Start Word and choose the **Blank Document** template.

2. If necessary, choose **Home→Paragraph→Show/Hide** ¶ to display nonprinting characters.

3. Tap Enter four times to move the insertion point down the page.

4. Choose **Home→Paragraph→Bullets** .

5. Type this list, tapping Enter at the end of lines when you need to generate a new bullet:

- **Separate your trash**
- **Always look for recycle bins**
- **Reuse shopping bags**
- **If it's broken, fix it**
- **Buy recycled products**
- **Take along reusable cups**
- **Use washable napkins**

6. Tap Enter three times to turn off bullets and add blank lines below the text. *You're adding space, because later you will add WordArt at the bottom of the page.*

7. Select the lines you typed.

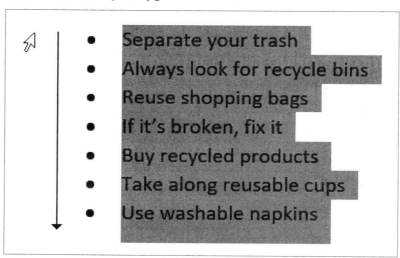

You will use Live Preview to explore a variety of fonts.

8. Make sure the Home tab is still active; if it isn't, click it.

9. Follow these steps to use Live Preview:

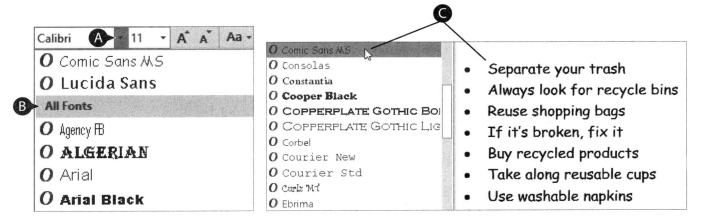

Ⓐ In the Font group, click the **Font menu** button ▾.

Ⓑ Scroll down to the **All Fonts** category. Fonts in this category are in alphabetical order.

Ⓒ Scroll down to Comic Sans MS and hover the mouse pointer over the font to observe the preview. Click **Comic Sans MS** to apply it to the selected lines.

Now you'll change the font size.

10. With the lines selected, follow these steps to change the font size:

Ⓐ Click the **Font Size menu** button ▾.

Ⓑ Choose **14** points.

Apply Formatting Using the Ribbon and Mini Toolbar

The Bold, Italic, and Underline buttons toggle on and off. That is, you click the Italic button to apply the italic format, and you click the same button to remove the format. The same is true for the Bold and Underline buttons.

11. With the lines still selected, choose **Home→Font→Italic** I.

12. Choose **Home→Font→Underline** U.

13. Click the **Italic** I button again to turn it off.

14. Click the **Underline** ☐U button again to turn it off.

Next you will use the Mini toolbar to turn on the Bold feature.

15. Click in the document to deselect the highlighted text.

16. Select the lines again and notice that the Mini toolbar appears.

17. Click the **Bold** ☐B button on the toolbar to apply bold to the selected text.

Now you will apply color to your text with the Mini toolbar.

18. Follow these steps to apply a shade of green to the text:

Ⓐ Click the **Font Color menu** button ▾.

Ⓑ Choose the last color in the last column: **Green, Accent 6, Darker 50%**.

Always leave your document open unless directed otherwise.

Saving a Document to a New Folder

A folder is an electronic location where you store groups of related files. So far, you have been storing files in the folders that relate to a chapter, such as the Chapter 04 folder. You can even create folders within folders for organizing your documents. It is easy to create folders using Word 2016. The Save As dialog box has a button for creating a new folder.

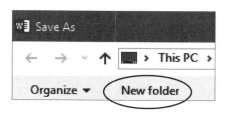

Naming Folders

Clicking the New Folder button creates a folder. The folder is temporarily named *New folder*, but the text is selected, so you can just type your new folder's name over the top of the highlighted text.

There are certain naming rules you must follow when you create a folder. If you try to give a folder a name that doesn't follow these rules, Word displays an error message.

RULES FOR NAMING FOLDERS

Rule	Description
Folder name length	A folder name can contain up to 255 characters.
Characters allowed in folder names	A folder name may contain alphabetic characters, numbers, spaces, periods, commas, semicolons, dashes, apostrophes, and parentheses.
Characters not allowed in folder names	A folder name *cannot* contain these characters: \ / : * ? " < > |

HANDS-ON 4.2 Create a Folder for Your Flyer

You know it's likely that you'll want to create more than one flyer for the recycling project, so in this exercise, you will create a new folder specifically for saving flyers.

1. Choose **File→Save As**.

2. Navigate to your **Chapter 04** folder and click the **New Folder** button at the top-left of the dialog box.

3. Type **Flyers** over the top of the highlighted *New folder* text and tap Enter.

4. Double-click the **folder** to open it.

5. Type **Recycle Flyer** in the File Name box at the bottom of the Save As dialog box and then click **Save**.

Setting Paragraph Alignment

Typically, you use paragraph alignment to align text between the margins of a document. You can also use it to align clip art and other graphic images. Paragraph alignment buttons are located in the Paragraph group of the Home tab. Alignment options include Align Left, Center, Align Right, and Justify.

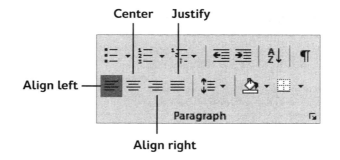

ALIGNMENT OPTIONS

Alignment	Example
Align Left aligns text with a straight left margin and a ragged right margin.	
Align Right aligns text with a ragged left margin and a straight right margin.	
Center centers text between the margins.	
Justify aligns text with straight left and right margins. Magazines and newspapers typically use justify.	

HANDS-ON 4.3 Set Paragraph Alignment

In this exercise, you will use the paragraph alignment buttons in the Paragraph group of the Home tab to align text between the margins.

1. Position the insertion point anywhere in a line of text.

2. Choose **Home→Paragraph→Center** ≡.
   The text is centered between the margins.

3. Choose **Home→Paragraph→Align Right** ≡.
   The text is now aligned with the right margin.

4. Choose **Home→Paragraph→Align Left** ≡ to align the text at the left margin.

Creating WordArt

WordArt is a graphic text image. You can format the image using a variety of shapes and colors. WordArt makes text look flashy—the perfect thing for a flyer. WordArt also makes interesting-looking document headings.

Reduce, Reuse, Recycle

Reduce, Reuse, Recycle

Reduce, Reuse, Recycle

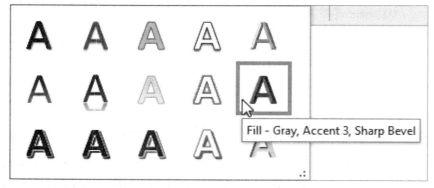 HANDS-ON 4.4 Insert WordArt

In this exercise, you will create a WordArt object by selecting a design from the WordArt gallery and typing the text that will appear in the object.

1. Press [Ctrl]+[Home] to position the insertion point at the top of the page.

2. Choose **Insert→Text→WordArt** ⓐ.

3. Choose the fifth style in the second row of the WordArt gallery.

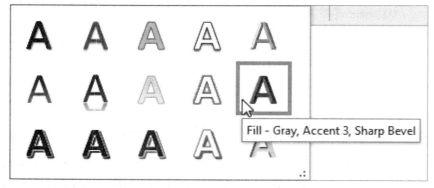

Fill - Gray, Accent 3, Sharp Bevel

A text box opens so you can type the flyer heading. Notice the small, circular handles surrounding the object, indicating that it's selected. You'll learn more about this in the next topic.

4. Type **Reduce, Reuse, Recycle** in the text box.

....

Formatting WordArt

You can format WordArt in a variety of ways. For example, you can change the shape, apply a 3-D style, and add shadow effects. This illustration shows an example of how to use Live Preview with the Bevel gallery to preview the formatting effect.

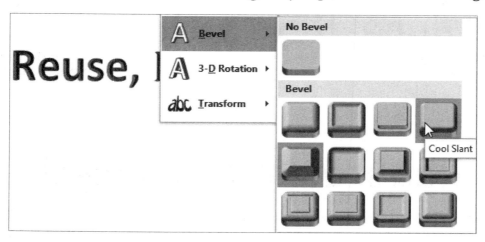

Contextual Tabs on the Ribbon

Contextual tabs appear in context with the task you are performing. When you select a WordArt object, the Drawing Tools' Format tab appears. Here you will find many features for formatting your WordArt.

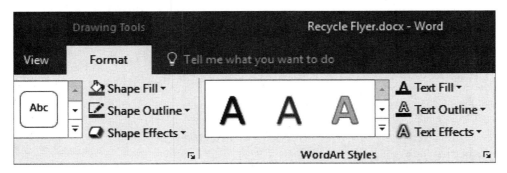

Selecting, Sizing, and Rotating WordArt

When you select a WordArt object, small circles known as *handles* surround it. When the insertion point is flashing in a word, only that word is selected; to select all words in the box, you need to click the box surrounding the object, which is made up of a dotted line (you have to look very carefully to see the dots) that changes to a solid line when clicked. Any formatting you then choose applies to all words.

The circular arrow at the top of the image is the rotate handle, which you can drag with the mouse pointer to rotate the image. You'll learn more about rotating images when you insert clip art later in this chapter.

When you position the mouse pointer on a handle, the pointer changes to a double-headed arrow that you can drag to increase or decrease the size of the object. Sizing using a corner handle changes the length and width relative to their original proportions.

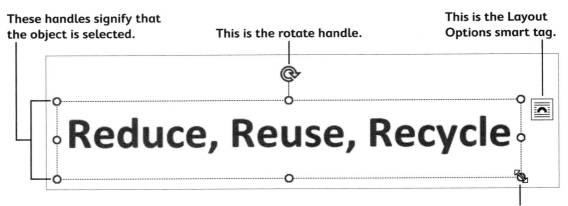

Note! You will not use the Layout Options smart tag with WordArt. You will use it later in the chapter; just ignore it for now.

HANDS-ON 4.5 Format WordArt

In this exercise, you will use the contextual Format tab to test a variety of formatting options including applying a Bevel effect.

1. Click the **border** of the WordArt text box.

   The line changes from dotted to solid, and the Drawing Tools' Format tab shows on the Ribbon.

2. Choose **Drawing Tools→Format→WordArt Styles→ Text Fill** ⓐ **menu button** ▾.

3. Choose the fifth color in the last column: **Green, Accent 6, Darker 25%**.

   Your heading now blends in with the bulleted text.

4. Choose **Drawing Tools→Format→WordArt Styles→Text Effects** ⓐ to display text-effect categories in the menu.

5. Slide the mouse pointer to the Shadow category and then hover (don't click) the mouse over several options to see the effects in Live Preview.

6. Use the same technique to explore the other categories.

   Remember: Don't click until you decide which effect you will use.

7. Move the mouse pointer to the Bevel category and choose **Cool Slant** (last option in the first row).

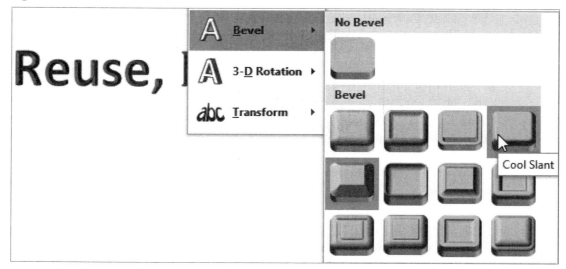

Now you will apply a Transform effect and resize the image.

8. Choose **Drawing Tools→Format→WordArt Styles→Text Effects** ⓐ.

9. Move the mouse pointer to the Transform category and choose **Chevron Up** in the Warp section.

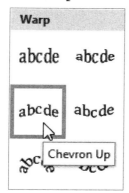

10. Position the mouse pointer on the circular handle on the right side.

    The mouse pointer changes to a double-headed arrow.

11. Press the mouse button.

    The pointer will change to a black cross when you start to drag.

12. Drag to the right until the right side of the text box is about an inch from the right edge of the page.

Add Another WordArt Image

13. Press Ctrl + End to position the insertion point below the bulleted text.

14. Choose **Insert→Text→WordArt** 4.

15. Click the last option in the first row: **Fill — Gold Accent 4, Soft Bevel**.

16. Type this in the text box: Do Your Part!

17. Click the **text box border** to select the entire object.

18. Choose **Drawing Tools→Format→WordArt Styles→ Text Fill** A **menu button** ▾.

19. Choose the fifth color in the last column: **Green, Accent 6, Darker 25%**.

20. Choose **Drawing Tools→Format→WordArt Styles→Text Effects** A.

21. In the Bevel category, choose **Cool Slant** (the last option in the first row).

22. Drag the **right-side handle** until the right edge of the text box is about an inch from the right edge of the page.

    This centers the text between the margins. Don't worry if the overall layout doesn't look right. You still need to add some clip art.

23. Save your flyer.

Using Clip Art and Pictures

Clip art adds excitement to your documents. You can browse through your computer or other computers to locate images for your document, or you can search online for images.

You can search for pictures saved as files on your computer.

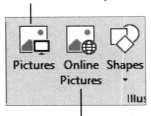

This option lets you search online for pictures and traditional clip art.

Use the Bing search box to search online for images.

Obeying Copyright Law

As per U.S. copyright law, it is illegal to use copyrighted pictures without the express consent of the copyright owner. This means you cannot simply search the Internet and use any picture you happen to find, as that picture may be protected by copyright. However, Word uses the Bing search engine to search for pictures online and by default displays only pictures licensed under Creative Commons, meaning you can use these pictures freely in your documents.

Rotating Clip Art

Clip art images have handles that work in a manner similar to WordArt handles. When you position the mouse pointer on a rotate handle, a circular arrow appears. You can then drag left or right to rotate the image.

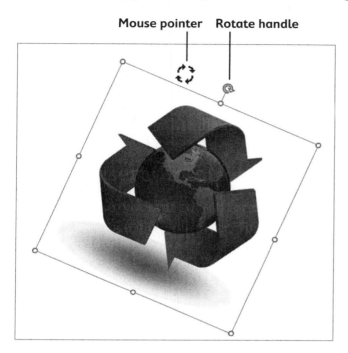

Mouse pointer   **Rotate handle**

Resizing Clip Art

You can change the size of clip art objects by dragging their handles like you did to resize a WordArt object. When you place the mouse pointer over a handle (other than the rotate handle), the pointer changes to a double-headed arrow. You then drag to resize the object.

Resizing from a side handle stretches or squeezes an image as you resize it, whereas resizing from a corner handle changes the height and width proportionally.

HANDS-ON 4.6 Insert, Rotate, and Resize Clip Art

In this exercise, you will search for a clip art image that's appropriate for the recycling project and place it in your flyer. Then you will rotate and resize the image.

1. Position the insertion point in the blank line below the flyer's heading.

2. Choose **Insert→Illustrations→Online Pictures** 🖼️.

3. If necessary, click in the **Bing search** box, type `recycle`, and tap Enter.

4. If necessary, scroll down and click this image to select it. (If you can't locate this image, choose another suitable image.)

5. Click **Insert** at the bottom-right corner.

6. If necessary, click the clip art image once to select it.

    The surrounding handles are visible when you select the clip art object. Notice the rotate handle at the top of the image.

7. Position the mouse pointer on the rotate handle, press and hold the mouse button, and drag to the left to rotate the image as shown; release the mouse button.

8. Click **Undo** ⤺ on the Quick Access toolbar to undo the rotation.

    Don't be concerned if the image changes position slightly after you click Undo.

9. Position the mouse pointer on the lower-right corner handle. When the mouse pointer changes to a double-headed arrow, drag until the image is about 4.5 inches wide.

    If you chose a clip art image other than the one shown, the final image size should be approximately 4.5 × 4.5 inches. Don't be overly concerned about the size. You can modify the size to your satisfaction at any time.

10. Save your file.

Layout Options

When an object is selected, a Layout Options smart tag appears to the right of it. Clicking the smart tag displays six text-wrapping options that determine how the surrounding text behaves relative to the object, such as square, top and bottom, and behind text.

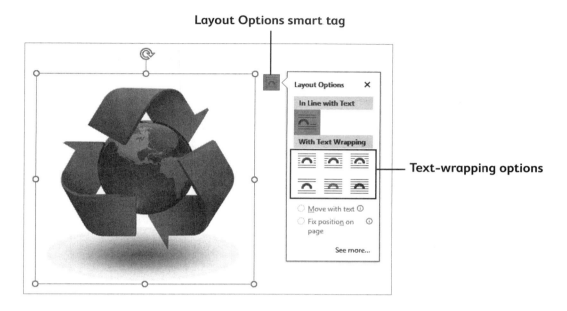

Layout Options smart tag

Text-wrapping options

Cropping Clip Art Images

Cropping allows you to hide parts of an image. You simply choose the Crop tool and drag one of the image's cropping handles to hide the unwanted portion of the image. Cropping does not affect the original image. The area hidden by cropping is not deleted, so you can uncrop an image, if necessary.

The cropped-off area

🖰 HANDS-ON 4.7 Wrap Text and Crop an Image

In this exercise, you will use the Square text-wrapping option with your clip art image and experiment with Live Preview. You will crop an image, and you will center the image and align the text on the page.

1. If necessary, click the **clip art image** to select it and display the Layout Options smart tag.

2. Follow these steps to apply text wrapping:

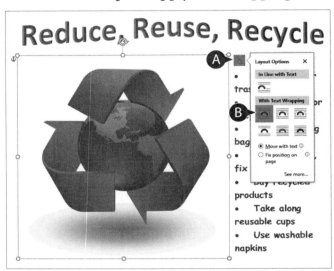

Ⓐ Click the **Layout Options** smart tag.

Ⓑ Choose **Square**.

3. Click in the document to view the effect of square wrapping.

   The image chosen and its sizing influence the wrapping effect. Now you'll position the image back in line with the text.

4. Select the object again and then click the **Layout Options** smart tag.

5. Choose **In Line with Text**.

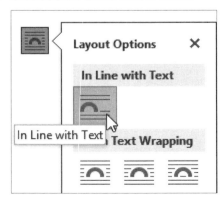

Crop and Uncrop the Image

Next you will crop some of the shadow from the bottom of the image. If you chose an image without a shadow, just clip a bit off the bottom of the image to get the experience of doing so.

6. Choose **Picture Tools→Format→Size→Crop** 🖼️.

7. Position the mouse pointer on the bottom-center thick, black handle.

   The mouse pointer looks like a thick, black T-shape.

8. Press and hold the mouse button and then drag up until about half of the shadow is cropped off; release the mouse button. If your image doesn't have a shadow, just drag up a bit.

9. Click in the document background to deselect the object and observe the effect of the cropping.

   You've decided you want to keep the shadow, so now you will uncrop the image.

10. Select the object again.

11. Choose **Picture Tools→Format→Size→Crop** 🖼️.

12. Position the mouse pointer on the black bottom-center handle.

13. Press and hold the mouse button and drag down until the shadow is visible again.

14. Release the mouse button.

    If the shadow is not completely visible, readjust the image with the Crop tool until you can see the entire shadow.

15. If necessary, choose **Picture Tools→Format→Size→Crop** 🖼️ to turn off the Crop tool.

    Now you will align the clip art image with the bullet points below it. You want the text to line up straight on the left, so you won't use the Center button, which would center each line between the margins individually. Instead you will use Tab to position the bullet points.

16. With the object selected, choose **Home→Paragraph→Center** ≡.

17. Select all seven lines of text and then tap Tab seven times.

    When you select several lines of text, using the Tab key moves all of the lines at once.

18. Save and close the file.

Self-Assessment

Check your knowledge of this chapter's key concepts and skills by completing the Self-Assessment.

Page number

1. When dealing with typography or working with word processors, font size is typically measured in points. **true false** _____

2. Live Preview shows how formatting changes look without actually applying the format. **true false** _____

3. Once you insert a WordArt image, you cannot change its shape. **true false** _____

4. A clip art image has a circular arrow rotate handle at its top. **true false** _____

5. Word allows you to wrap text around a clip art image. **true false** _____

6. Paragraph alignment works for text but not for graphic images. **true false** _____

7. You know a WordArt image is selected when _____.

   A. the handles are visible

   B. it is highlighted

   C. the WordArt task pane appears

   D. it is visible from the Print command in Backstage view

   Page number: _____

8. Which of the following statements regarding cropping an image is correct?

   A. Cropping hides part of an image.

   B. Once you crop an image, you cannot recover the cropped portion.

   C. You cannot crop clip art images that you find on the Internet.

   D. The cropping tool is in the Layout Options smart tag.

   Page number: _____

9. Layout Options allow you to _____.

   A. keep typing in a paragraph without tapping Enter

   B. wrap text around a graphic image

   C. create a master layout plan

   D. rotate a graphic image

   Page number: _____

10. The Mini toolbar _____.

   A. contains frequently used formatting commands

   B. is located on the contextual Format tab

   C. always appears at the bottom of the Word window

   D. contains the Layout Options feature

   Page number: _____

Skill Builders

SKILL BUILDER 4.1 **Create WordArt and Format Text**

You are a teaching assistant in the Physical Education Department at Central College. The instructor heard that you are producing some interesting documents with Word, and she asks for your help. In this exercise, you will format the martial arts course description flyer that will be available when students sign up for classes.

Note! Turn the Show/Hide ¶ button on or off as you prefer.

1. Open **sb-Martial Arts Schedule** from your **Chapter 04** folder.
   You'll use WordArt to format the first line of the document. Since the text is already typed, you can just select it and apply the WordArt style.

2. Select the first line in the document.

3. Choose **Insert→Text→WordArt** 𝒜 .

4. Choose the first WordArt style in the first row: **Fill – Black, Text 1, Shadow**.
   Now you will apply a text effect to the WordArt image.

5. Choose **Drawing Tools→Format→WordArt Styles→Text Effects** 𝔸 .

6. Slide the mouse pointer down to the Glow category and choose the third variation in the first row.

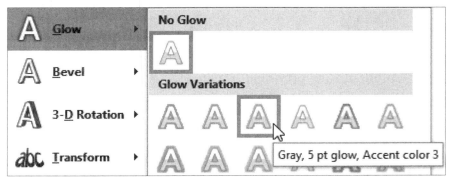

Now you will resize the WordArt image and add fill color.

7. Place the mouse pointer on the right-side handle and drag to the right until the text fits on one line.

8. If necessary, position the mouse pointer on the border of the WordArt object (the mouse pointer appears as a four-headed arrow) and drag the object to center it between the margins.

9. Choose **Drawing Tools→Format→WordArt Styles→ Text Fill △ menu button ▾**.

10. Choose the color in the fifth column, fifth row.

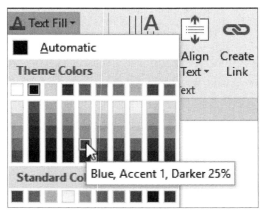

Format Text with the Ribbon and the Mini Toolbar

11. Select the lines *Fall Semester Schedule* and *Martial Arts Courses*.

12. Choose **Home→Font→Font Size menu button ▾** and choose **16** point font.

13. Choose **Home→Paragraph→Center ≡**.

14. Select the first course name, *Kung Fu Level 1*, and apply **12** point **Tahoma** font.

15. Select the line again to display the Mini toolbar.

16. Click the **Bold B** button on the Mini toolbar.
    The toolbar remains open.

17. Click the **Font Color △ menu** button ▾ and choose the color in the fifth column, fifth row: **Blue**, **Accent 1**, **Darker 25%**.
    The Font Color button remembers the last color you chose from the menu, and that color appears on the button face. You can repeat the color without opening the menu by clicking the button face.

18. Format the other three course names using the same attributes: **12** point **Tahoma Bold** and the same shade of blue.

19. Select the first line below the heading *King Fu Level 1* and apply the **Arial** font.

20. Repeat the **Arial** formatting for the first line below the other three course headings.

21. Save and close the file.

SKILL BUILDER 4.2 Work with Clip Art and Create a Folder

It's time for the annual science fair at the school where you are student teaching. In this exercise, you will help a student create a flyer to use as a handout for his project. You'll begin by inserting clip art.

1. Open **sb-Carbon Footprint** from your **Chapter 04** folder.

2. If necessary, choose **Home→Paragraph→Show/Hide** ¶ to display nonprinting characters.

3. Position the insertion point next to the second paragraph symbol below the WordArt heading.

4. Choose **Insert→Illustrations→Online Pictures** 🖼.

5. Follow these steps to search for clip art:

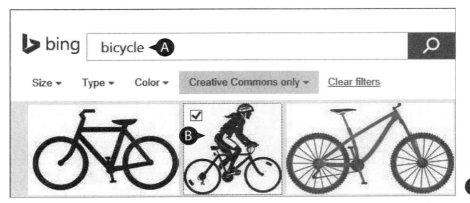

Ⓐ Type **bicycle** in the search box and tap [Enter].

Ⓑ Click this image. (If you can't locate this image, choose an appropriate bicycle image.)

Ⓒ Click **Insert**.

6. If necessary, click the image to select it.

   Now you will resize, rotate, and center the clip art.

7. Position the mouse pointer on the image's bottom-right handle.

   The mouse pointer changes to a double-headed arrow.

8. Drag down and to the right about an inch to make the image a bit larger; release the mouse button.

   If you chose a different image, resize it to fit nicely on one page.

   Next you will center the image between the margins.

9. With the image selected, choose **Home**→**Paragraph**→**Center** ☰.

   Now you will rotate the clip art. The circular arrow rotate handle is visible at the top of the image.

10. Place the mouse pointer on the rotate handle.

    The pointer changes to a circular arrow.

11. Drag the handle to the left until the image is rotated to approximately the same degree as shown.

Save the Flyer in a New Folder

12. Choose **File**→**Save As**.

13. Navigate to your **Chapter 04** folder and click the **New Folder** button at the top of the dialog box.

14. Name the folder `Science Projects` and tap Enter.

15. Double-click the folder to open it and then click **Save**.

16. Close the flyer.

SKILL BUILDER 4.3 Use Layout Options with Clip Art

In this exercise, you will insert a clip art image in a document and experiment with wrapping text and positioning the image.

1. Open **sb-Photographs** from your **Chapter 04** folder.

2. Position the insertion point at the beginning of the first main paragraph.

3. Choose **Insert→Illustrations→Online Pictures** 🖼.

4. Follow these steps to search for clip art:

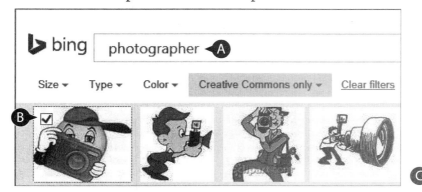

Ⓐ Type **photographer** in the search box and tap Enter.

Ⓑ Click this image. (If you can't locate this image, choose an appropriate photographer image.)

Ⓒ Click **Insert**.

5. Resize the image to about 2 inches wide by 1.5 inches high.

6. Make sure the image is selected.

7. Click the **Layout Options** smart tag and choose **Square**.

8. Try out several other layout options and then choose **Square** again.

9. Position the mouse pointer on the image's border (the mouse pointer appears as a four-headed arrow) and drag it to the right until it's positioned as shown.

PHOTOGRAPHS

If you are including professional photographs in your flyers, especially of people, there are a few guidelines that will make your publication easier and more attractive. Before you choose a photographer, do your homework. Ask your friends and fellow professionals for referrals. Go see several photographers. You should ask to see a portfolio of their work. Tell them what you want and what you are going to use the photos for.

10. Save and close the file.

11. Exit Word.

Tracking Firefighter Training

Excel is an exciting tool that can perform many tasks, including organizing lists of information, crunching numbers, and creating charts. Organizing lists is a database function. An Excel database is an electronic version of a paper filing system. Examples of databases include name and address lists, patient records, and inventory lists. In Excel, you can quickly sort information alphabetically, numerically, and by date. In this chapter, you will use a database to explore Excel basics such as navigating, entering, and editing data.

LEARNING OBJECTIVES

- Identify the important parts of an Excel window
- Navigate in a spreadsheet and freeze panes
- Enter and edit data
- Move, copy, and sort data
- Insert, delete, and resize columns and rows

Project: Creating a Training Database

You are an administrator at a fire department in your county. The chief has asked you to set up a training database for firefighters and emergency personnel. You find that Excel is a first-rate tool for the job because it allows you to sort the database on any column; this is particularly helpful for organizing data in the various ways the chief requests.

Last Name	First Name	Hire Date	Rank	Shift
Alexander	Martin	3/24/1999	Firefighter/EMT-Paramedic	3
Bryan	Henry	3/13/1996	Firefighter	2
Cooper	Douglas	2/12/2013	EMT-Paramedic	2
Elizondo	Jose	1/27/1992	Firefighter/EMT-Paramedic	2
Ellis	Gregory	8/14/1992	Firefighter/EMT-Intermediate	1
Frost	Suzanne	5/19/1996	Firefighter/EMT-Basic	1

Sorted by the Last Name column

Last Name	First Name	Hire Date	Rank	Shift
Smith	Anthony	12/16/1991	Firefighter/EMT-Basic	3
Elizondo	Jose	1/27/1992	Firefighter/EMT-Paramedic	2
Ellis	Gregory	8/14/1992	Firefighter/EMT-Intermediate	1
Paulson	Glenn	6/15/1993	Firefighter	1
Jensen	Oliver	8/25/1994	EMT-Intermediate	2

Sorted by the Hire Date column

Last Name	First Name	Hire Date	Rank	Shift
Ellis	Gregory	8/14/1992	Firefighter/EMT-Intermediate	1
Paulson	Glenn	6/15/1993	Firefighter	1
Malik	Hasan	12/4/1995	Firefighter	1
Frost	Suzanne	5/19/1996	Firefighter/EMT-Basic	1
Morgan	Jack	8/1/1996	Firefighter	1

Sorted by the Shift column

What Is Excel?

Excel 2016 is a spreadsheet (or worksheet) program that is part of the Microsoft Office 2016 suite of software programs. A spreadsheet program allows you to organize data in columns and rows as well as to analyze the data and perform calculations on it. There are three kinds of entries in spreadsheets: text, numbers, and formulas.

You can use spreadsheets to create a variety of files, including income statements, financial statements, budgets, databases, and invoices.

The Excel Start Screen

The Excel Start screen is the first screen you see when you start the program. It offers several ways to begin working. Don't be concerned if your Start screen is arranged differently from that shown in this example. If it looks different, it might be because a previous user rearranged the templates on the right side of the screen or because your screen's resolution differs.

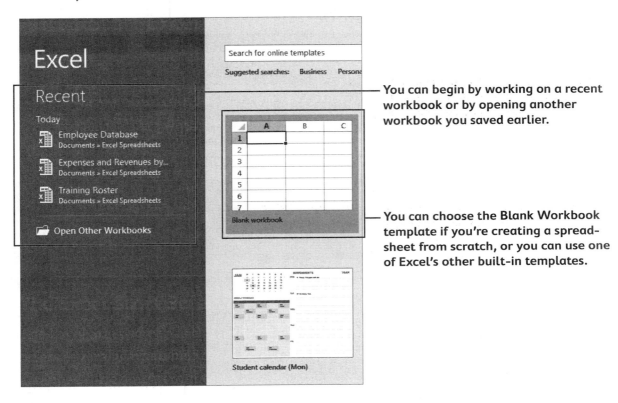

You can begin by working on a recent workbook or by opening another workbook you saved earlier.

You can choose the Blank Workbook template if you're creating a spreadsheet from scratch, or you can use one of Excel's other built-in templates.

HANDS-ON 5.1 Start Excel

In this exercise, you will start the Excel program.

1. If necessary, start your computer.

2. Click the **Start** button in the bottom-left corner of the screen.

3. Scroll down the alphabetical list and click **Excel 2016**.
   The Excel program loads and the Start screen appears.

4. **Maximize** the Excel window if it isn't already maximized.

5. Click the **Blank Workbook** template to open the Excel window.
   Always leave your file open unless directed otherwise.

The Excel 2016 Window

Excel opens with a new, blank workbook that allows you to enter and analyze data, and to maintain lists of information. There are a number of similarities between the Word window and the Excel window. For example, both windows have a File tab, a Ribbon, and a Quick Access toolbar.

The Suite Advantage

Now you're starting to see the advantage of working with a suite of software programs. When you learn one program, you're a step ahead when it's time to learn the next one.

Don't be concerned if your workbook window looks slightly different from that in the example. Just as in Word, the Excel screen is customizable.

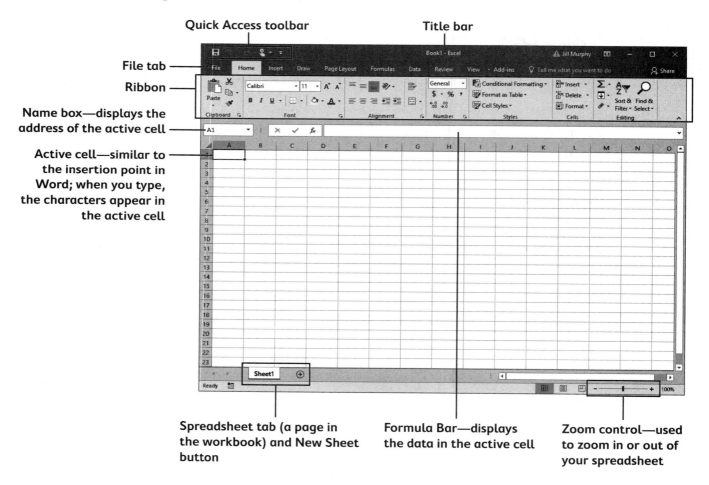

Quick Access toolbar

Title bar

File tab

Ribbon

Name box—displays the address of the active cell

Active cell—similar to the insertion point in Word; when you type, the characters appear in the active cell

Spreadsheet tab (a page in the workbook) and New Sheet button

Formula Bar—displays the data in the active cell

Zoom control—used to zoom in or out of your spreadsheet

Workbook Organization

An Excel file is often referred to as a *workbook*. That's because, like a book, it's made up of pages. These pages are known as *spreadsheets* or *worksheets* (see the Sheet 1 tab in the previous illustration).

Spreadsheet

A spreadsheet is made up of a series of columns and rows. The columns are headed with alphabetical characters, and the rows are headed with numbers. There are 16,384 columns and 1,048,576 rows. (That's probably more room than you will ever need!) Since there are only twenty-six letters in the alphabet, when Excel gets to column Z, it starts over, labeling the columns with AA, AB, AC, and all the way through AZ before moving on to BA, BB, BC, and so forth.

Defining Cells

A small rectangle appears wherever a column and row intersect. These rectangles are known as *cells*. All cells have addresses that are determined by the column and row indicators. The address of the first cell in the upper-left corner of the spreadsheet—in column A and row 1—is A1. A1 is the active cell in the illustration; the active cell has a dark border around it. When you type data, it automatically goes into the active cell.

The address of the active cell appears in the Name box at the left end of the Formula Bar.

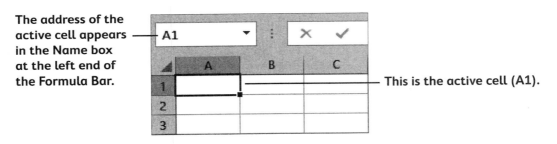

This is the active cell (A1).

Mouse Shapes in Excel

The mouse pointer in Excel takes on many different forms, depending on what you are doing. Excel behaves differently relative to the mouse pointer shape.

EXCEL MOUSE POINTER SHAPES

Mouse Shape	Purpose
✛	The thick, white cross appears when the pointer is over a cell. Clicking with this pointer selects a cell; clicking and dragging selects a range of cells.
+	The AutoFill handle (a small, black cross) appears when the mouse pointer is on the tiny square (fill handle) in the bottom-right corner of a selected cell. Dragging the fill handle copies cells or generates a data series (such as 1, 2, 3, 4, etc.) to adjacent cells.
⬉	The mouse pointer looks like a white arrow when moved over the Ribbon or when you use the scroll bars.
✥	The move pointer appears when the mouse pointer is hovered over the edge of a cell or cell range (except in the bottom-right corner). Clicking and dragging cells allows you to move them to a new location.
↔	The mouse pointer changes to the resize pointer when placed between row or column headers. Clicking and dragging it allows you to change the size of rows or columns. Double-clicking it makes a row or column as tall or wide as its tallest or widest entry.
→1	When the mouse pointer is on a row header, it changes to a right-pointing arrow. Clicking it selects the entire row.
↓A	Placing the mouse pointer on a column header changes the pointer to a down-pointing arrow. Clicking it selects the entire column.
I	The I-beam appears when you are entering or editing text in the Formula Bar or within a cell.

Navigating in Excel

If you are working with a large spreadsheet, it's convenient to know some techniques for moving around quickly. There are a number of mouse moves and keyboard techniques you can use, some of which are the same as those used in Word.

The Scroll Bars

When you navigate using scroll bars, the active cell does not move. After scrolling, you must click in the spreadsheet to reposition the active cell. You can see in the illustration that scrolling in Excel is similar to scrolling in Word.

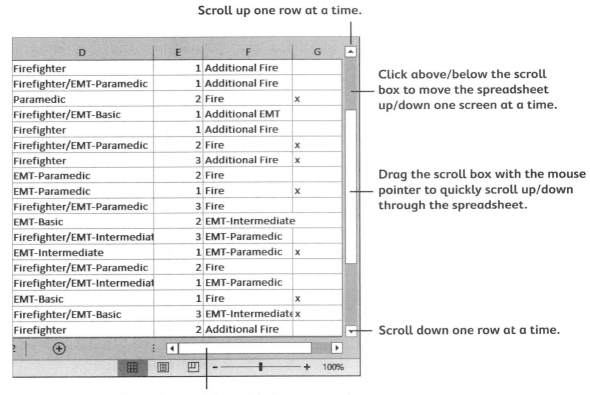

Scroll up one row at a time.

Click above/below the scroll box to move the spreadsheet up/down one screen at a time.

Drag the scroll box with the mouse pointer to quickly scroll up/down through the spreadsheet.

Scroll down one row at a time.

Drag the scroll box with the mouse pointer to quickly scroll right/left through the spreadsheet.

HANDS-ON 5.2 Scroll in a Spreadsheet

In this exercise, you will close the blank workbook, open another workbook, and scroll in a spreadsheet.

1. Choose **File→Close** and then choose **File→Open**.

2. Navigate to the **Chapter 05** folder and open **Training Roster**.

3. Follow these steps to use the scroll bar to navigate within the spreadsheet:

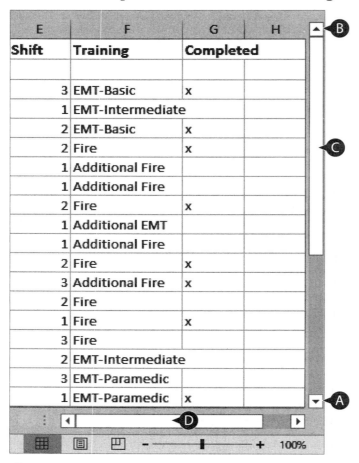

Ⓐ Click the **scroll down** button to move down one row. Press and hold the mouse button to rapidly scroll down.

Ⓑ Click the **scroll up** button once to move up one row. Press and hold the mouse button to rapidly scroll up.

Ⓒ Hold the mouse button and drag the **scroll box** down to quickly move down the spreadsheet. (The change is not dramatic since the spreadsheet is not very long.) Drag the **scroll box** to the top of the scroll bar.

Ⓓ Try similar techniques using the horizontal scroll bar.

Notice that the active cell does not change position when you scroll through a spreadsheet.

The Keyboard

If your hands are on the keyboard, it may be faster to use the keyboard navigation shortcuts provided by Excel. Unlike when scrolling, when you navigate using the keyboard, the active cell moves with you.

EXCEL KEYBOARD NAVIGATION TECHNIQUES

Command	Description
Ctrl + Home	Moves to cell A1
Ctrl + End	Moves to the end of the data in the spreadsheet
Home	Moves to the beginning of the row
Page Down	Moves down one screen
Page Up	Moves up one screen
→ ← ↑ ↓	Moves one cell to the right, left, up, or down

HANDS-ON 5.3 Navigate with the Keyboard

In this exercise, you will use keyboard techniques to move around a spreadsheet.

1. Tap the arrow keys → ← ↓ ↑ on the keyboard a few times to move through the spreadsheet.

2. Press and hold the **down arrow** ↓ to produce a repeat action effect.
   All four arrow keys perform a repeat action if you hold them down.

3. Press Ctrl + Home to move to **cell A1**.
   Do you remember the same keystrokes in Word? You're getting twice the benefit from one learned task.

4. Tap Ctrl + End to move to the end of the data in the spreadsheet.

5. Tap Home to move to the beginning of the row.

6. Press Ctrl + Home to move back to **cell A1**.

Freezing Panes

You may have a spreadsheet so long that when you scroll down to see the last row of data, the headings at the tops of the columns scroll off the screen, and this can make it difficult to understand the meaning of data. The same is true of a wide spreadsheet and row headings; scrolling to the right could cause the row headings to disappear, again making it difficult to understand what the data represents.

Freezing columns and rows allows you to keep the column and row headings visible while examining data in any part of the spreadsheet—even data that is not close to the headings.

FREEZING COLUMNS AND ROWS

Command	Description
Freeze Top Row	As you scroll down the spreadsheet, the top row remains visible. The top row is whatever row appears at the top of the screen when you freeze panes; it may not be row 1.
Freeze First Column	As you scroll to the right, the first column remains visible. The first column is whatever column appears at the left edge of the screen when you freeze panes; it may not be column A.
Freeze Panes	Select a cell and choose the Freeze Panes command to freeze everything above and to the left of the selected cell.
Unfreeze Panes	This command unlocks the frozen columns and/or rows.

HANDS-ON 5.4 Freeze Panes

In this exercise, you will freeze rows and columns so they remain static when you scroll in the spreadsheet.

1. Scroll down the spreadsheet until the column headings disappear off the screen.
   Without the column headings, it's difficult to understand the meaning of the data.

2. Press ⸢Ctrl⸣+⸢Home⸣ to move to **cell A1**.
   Now you will freeze the first row.

3. Choose **View→Window→Freeze Panes** and then choose **Freeze Top Row**.
   Notice the darker line that appears below row 1, indicating that the freeze action is in effect.

Tip! The *top row* is the row that happens to appear at the top of the screen at the time you choose Freeze Top Row from the menu; it won't necessarily be row 1.

4. Follow these steps to see the effect of freezing the top row:

▲	A	B	C	D
1	Last Name	First Name		Rank ◄ Ⓑ
16	Alexander	Martin		Firefighter/EMT-Paramedic
17	Mahal	Jasleen		EMT-Basic
18	Wright	Roger		Firefighter/EMT-Intermediate
19	Webster	Alan		EMT-Intermediate
20	Penbrook	Robert		Firefighter/EMT-Paramedic
21	Schultz	Edward		Firefighter/EMT-Intermediate
22	Waldek	John		EMT-Basic
23	Smith	Anthony		Firefighter/EMT-Basic
24	Swan	Edwin		Firefighter
25	Iverson	George		Firefighter/EMT-Basic

Ⓐ Scroll down the screen until **row 16** is just below **row 1**.

Ⓑ Notice that the column headings in **row 1** are still visible, making the meaning of the data easy to understand.

5. Scroll to the top of the spreadsheet.

Now you will freeze the first column.

6. Choose **View→Window→Freeze Panes** 🗗 and then choose **Freeze First Column**.

This unfreezes the first row and freezes the first column. Notice that the darker line is no longer below row 1 and instead appears to the right of column A.

Tip! The first column is the column that happens to appear at the left edge of the screen at the time you choose Freeze First Column; it won't necessarily be column A.

7. Scroll to the right and notice that the first column remains in place.

Now you will unfreeze the panes.

8. Choose **View→Window→Freeze Panes** 🗗 and then choose **Unfreeze Panes**.

The darker line to the right of column A disappears.

Freeze Columns and Rows at the Same Time

9. Select **cell D2** to make it the active cell.

10. Choose **View→Window→Freeze Panes** 🗗 and then choose **Freeze Panes**.

Notice the darker horizontal and vertical lines that indicate everything above and to the left of the active cell, cell D2, is frozen.

11. Follow these steps to scroll in both directions:

	A	B	C	⬤B F	G
1	Last Name	First Name		Training	Completed
⬤A 5	Bryan	Henry		EMT-Basic	x
6	Jensen	Oliver		Fire	x
7	Paulson	Glenn		Additional Fire	
8	Sanchez	Barbara		Additional Fire	
9	Gordon	Maxwell		Fire	x
10	Frost	Suzanne		Additional EMT	
11	Morgan	Jack		Additional Fire	

Ⓐ Scroll down until **row 5** is just below **row 1**.

Ⓑ Scroll right until **column F** is next to **column C**.

12. Choose **View→Window→Freeze Panes** 🔳 and then choose **Unfreeze Panes**.

- -

Entering Data in a Spreadsheet

Now that you're getting comfortable with spreadsheet terminology and navigation, it's time to enter data so you can keep the training roster up to date.

When you start to enter data in a spreadsheet, the Cancel and Enter buttons at the left side of the Formula Bar appear bolder, indicating that you are in the process of entering data.

Cancel

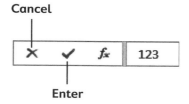

Enter

Completing and Canceling Entries

Entering data is a two-step process. Once you type data in a cell, the next step is to complete the entry. If you suddenly realize that you selected the wrong cell, you may want to cancel the entry.

COMPLETING AND CANCELING CELL ENTRIES

Method	Result
Tap [Enter]	Excel completes the entry; the active cell moves down one row.
Tap [Tab]	Excel completes the entry; the active cell moves to the right one column.
Tap an arrow key on the keyboard	Excel completes the entry; the active cell moves in the direction of the arrow.
Click the Enter button on the Formula Bar	Excel completes the entry; the active cell remains active.
Click the Cancel button on the Formula Bar	Excel removes any data typed in the cell; the active cell remains active.
Tap [Esc]	Excel removes any data typed in the cell; the active cell remains active.

HANDS-ON 5.5 Enter Data

In this exercise, you will enter data about a new firefighter in a roster spreadsheet using several data entry techniques.

1. Follow these steps to enter data in the spreadsheet:

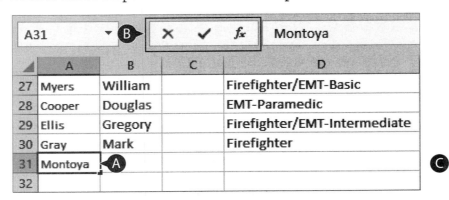

Ⓐ Select **cell A31** and type **Montoya**. Don't tap [Enter] yet.

Ⓑ Notice that the Cancel and Enter buttons appear bold on the Formula Bar. This means you have not completed the entry.

Ⓒ Tap [Enter] to finish entering the data.

The Cancel and Enter buttons appear lighter, and the active cell moves down one row.

2. Select **cell A31** again and look at the Formula Bar.

You see that the data you entered appears in the Formula Bar as well as in the cell. Later in this chapter, you will use the Formula Bar to make editing changes.

3. Follow these steps to enter data in **cell B31**:

	A	B	C	D
27	Myers	William		Firefighter/EMT-Basic
28	Cooper	Douglas		EMT-Paramedic
29	Ellis	Gregory		Firefighter/EMT-Intermediate
30	Gray	Mark		Firefighter
31	Montoya	Margarita		
32				

B31 — X **(B)** ✓ *fx* Margarita

(A) Select **cell B31** and type **Margarita**, but don't tap Enter .

(B) Click the **Enter** button to complete the entry.

Cell B31 remains the active cell when you use the Enter button.

4. Select **cell D31**, type **Firefighter**, and tap ↓ to complete the entry.

Tapping ↓ has the same effect as tapping Enter : The active cell moves down one row. Cell D32 is now the active cell.

5. Select **cell E31**, type **3**, and complete the entry by tapping Tab .

This moves the active cell one column to the right and makes cell F31 the active cell. You will enter the term Fire *in cell F31. Because the word* Fire *already appears in column F, Excel will use AutoComplete (similar to Word) to enter the term for you.*

6. Type **F** in **cell F31** and watch as Excel autocompletes *Fire*.

7. Tap Tab to complete the entry.

Tip! If you want to type something other than what Excel proposes, just keep typing.

8. Save the file.

· ·

QUICK REFERENCE: Deleting, Replacing, and Editing Data

Task	Procedure
Delete an entry	Select the cell and tap Delete .
Replace an entry	Select the cell, type the new data, and complete the entry.
Edit text in the Formula Bar	Select the cell to make its data appear in the Formula Bar, click to place the insertion point in the Formula Bar, and then modify the data.
Use in-cell editing	Double-click the cell to place the insertion point in it. Modify the data in the cell.

🖱 HANDS-ON 5.6 Edit Data

In this exercise, you will use different editing techniques to modify your spreadsheet. You realize that Mark Gray (row 30) did not complete his Additional Fire training yet, so the first thing you will do is delete the "x" in cell G30.

1. Select **cell G30** and tap [Delete].

   Oliver Jensen's last name is incorrect; it should be Jensen, *not* Justin *(row 6).*

2. Select **cell A6**, type **Jensen**, and tap [Enter].

   The correct name replaces the original entry. Next you will correct Oliver's title by adding the word Firefighter *in front of* EMT-Intermediate, *editing it in the Formula Bar.*

3. Follow these steps to make the correction:

D6	▼	⋮	✕	✓	*fx* Ⓒ ▶ EMT-Intermediate ◀ Ⓑ	

◢	A	B	C	D	E
1	**Last Name**	**First Name**		**Rank**	**Shift**
2					
3	Harrington	John		Firefighter	3
4	Kashner	Kevin		Firefighter/EMT-Basic	1
5	Bryan	Henry		EMT-Basic	2
6	Jensen	Oliver	Ⓐ	EMT-Intermediate	2
7	Paulson	Glenn		Firefighter	1

   Ⓐ Select **cell D6**.

   Ⓑ Notice that the data appears in the Formula Bar. You will make the correction there.

   Ⓒ Click in front of the term *EMT*, type **Firefighter/**, and tap [Enter].

   Because Oliver is already a firefighter, he doesn't need Fire training; he needs Additional Fire training. This time you will make the editing change directly in the cell.

4. Double-click **cell F6**.

   This places the insertion point in the cell and causes the mouse pointer to change to an I-beam.

5. If necessary, click in front of *Fire.* Type **Additional**, tap [Spacebar], and tap [Tab].

   The active cell is now cell G6. Oliver has not completed the Additional Fire training.

6. Tap [Delete] to remove the "x" from **cell G6**.

7. Save the file.

Aligning Cell Contents

By default, Excel aligns text to the left edges of cells and numbers to the right edges of cells. You can use the alignment buttons on the Ribbon to modify alignment within cells. They function in a manner similar to the alignment buttons in Word: Align Left, Center, and Align Right.

🖱 HANDS-ON 5.7 Align Data in Cells

In this exercise, you will use the alignment buttons to change the alignment of data in your spreadsheet.

1. Select **cell D1**.

2. Choose **Home→Alignment→Align Right** ≡.

3. Choose **Home→Alignment→Center** ≡.

4. Select **cell E1**.

5. Choose **Home→Alignment→Center** ≡.

6. Center the text in **cell F1**.

7. Save the file.

Working with Cell Ranges

A cell range is a group of adjacent cells. You select (highlight) cell ranges when you want to do something with them, such as formatting, moving, or copying them. You can also use cell ranges in formulas, which you will learn about later in the course.

You identify cell ranges by the cell addresses in the upper-left and lower-right corners of the range. A colon is placed between the two cell addresses, such as A1:C10. This is described as A1 *through* C10.

When you select a range of cells, a white cell appears in the upper-left corner of the range. This is the active cell. If you type data, it will appear in the white cell.

Task	Procedure
Select a range	- Option 1: Select the first cell in the range, press the mouse button, and drag to the last cell. - Option 2: Select the first cell in the range, press ⎡Shift⎤, and click the last cell in the range. - Option 3: Click the first cell in the range, hold down ⎡Shift⎤, and tap the arrow keys to select the range.
Select a column	- Click the column header; for example, to select column A, click directly on the *A* at the top of the column.
Select a row	- Click the row header; for example, to select row 1, click directly on the *1* at the beginning of the row.
Select the entire spreadsheet	- Click the Select All button (between the row 1 header and the column A header) in the upper-left corner of the spreadsheet.

HANDS-ON 5.8 Select Ranges of Cells

In this exercise, you will use several techniques for selecting cell ranges.

1. Follow these steps to select the **range A1:E9**:

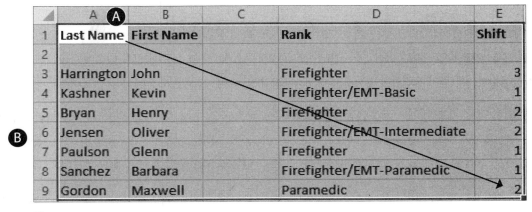

Ⓐ Position the mouse pointer in **cell A1**, press the mouse button, and drag down to the right to **cell E9**.

Ⓑ Release the mouse button to select the range. If you make a mistake, click anywhere in the spreadsheet to deselect the range and try again.

2. Click any cell to deselect the range.

3. Select **cell A1**.

4. Hold down $\boxed{\text{Shift}}$ and click **cell E9** to select the **range A1:E9**.

5. Click any cell to deselect the range.

Select a Range Using Arrow Keys

6. Click **cell A1** and then hold down $\boxed{\text{Shift}}$ and tap $\boxed{\rightarrow}$ four times to select through **column E**.

7. While holding down $\boxed{\text{Shift}}$, tap $\boxed{\downarrow}$ enough times to highlight through **row 9**.
   Notice that the highlighting of the row headers and column headers helps you see which rows and columns you selected.

8. Click any cell to deselect the range.
   Next you will select column D. When you select a column, the mouse pointer looks like a down-pointing black arrow.

9. Place the mouse pointer over the column header for **column D** and click.

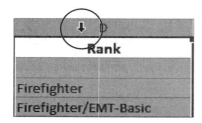

   This selects the entire column—all the way down to row 1,048,576.

10. Place the mouse pointer over the row header for **row 1** and click.

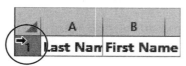

   This selects the entire row—all the way over to column 16,384.

11. Click the **Select All** button.

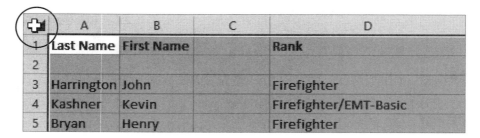

   This selects the entire spreadsheet.

12. Press $\boxed{\text{Ctrl}}$ + $\boxed{\text{Home}}$ to deselect and make **cell A1** the active cell.

Moving and Copying Data

Moving and copying data in a spreadsheet eliminates the need to retype it, thus saving time. When you move data, you remove it from its original position and place it in a new one. When you copy data, the original remains in place while a copy of the data is placed in a new location.

QUICK REFERENCE: Moving and Copying Data with Cut, Copy, and Paste

Task	Procedure
Move data	▪ Select the cell(s) you want to move and then click the Cut button.
	▪ Click the destination cell and then click the Paste button.
Copy data	▪ Select the cell(s) you want to copy and then click the Copy button.
	▪ Click the destination cell and then click the Paste button.

HANDS-ON 5.9 Move and Copy Data

In this exercise, you will use the Cut, Copy, and Paste buttons to move and copy data.

1. Follow these steps to move data from **column F** to **column I**:

   Ⓐ Select the **range F1:F10**.

   Ⓑ Choose **Home→Clipboard→Cut**.

    A flashing marquee surrounds the cut cells to indicate that you are in the process of moving them.

   Ⓒ Select **cell I1**.

   Ⓓ Choose **Home→Clipboard→Paste**.

    The data moves from the original range to the new range. At this point there should be no data in the range F1:F10.

2. Follow these steps to copy data from **column I** to **column K**:

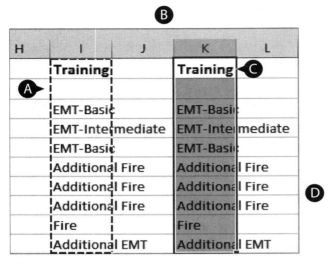

Ⓐ If necessary, select the range **I1:I10**.

Ⓑ Choose **Home→Clipboard→Copy**.

Ⓒ Select **cell K1**.

Ⓓ Choose **Home→Clipboard→Paste**.

Because you copied the data instead of moving it, the data is visible in both columns I and K.

The flashing marquee will disappear as you work in the spreadsheet; however, you can make it go away at any time by tapping the Esc *key.*

3. If desired, tap Esc .

4. Save the file.

Sorting Data

Organizing data in a logical sequence often makes the data easier to understand and work with. Sorting information alphabetically or numerically is one of the primary capabilities of a spreadsheet program like Excel. This also means that you can create lists randomly, placing all new entries at the bottom of the list and then asking Excel to sort the list for you.

Kinds of Sorts

The kind of sort Excel offers to perform is based on the type of data in the column by which you want to sort. If you select a cell in a text column, Excel offers to sort from A to Z or from Z to A. If the column contains only numbers, Excel proposes sorting from smallest to largest or from largest to smallest. If the column is populated with dates, Excel will suggest sorting from oldest to newest or from newest to oldest.

Alphabetical sort options

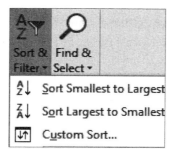

Numeric sort options

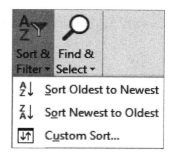

Date sort options

Structuring an Effective List

There are a few things you should keep in mind when creating a list that you can sort effectively.

- **No blanks:** There can be no blank columns or rows in a list. Blanks can cause serious problems when sorting a list. All data must be adjacent. (It's fine to have blank cells *within* a column/row, but the entire column or row cannot be blank.)

- **Consistent terminology:** This ensures that items that are meant to sort together stay together. For example, if you are a car dealer and you sell SUVs, you shouldn't refer to such vehicles as an *SUV* in one row and as a *sport utility* in another row. Excel does not consider these two terms to be the same.

 HANDS-ON 5.10 **Sort Data**

In this exercise, you will perform an alphabetical sort, a numeric sort, and a date sort. You will begin by switching to the Sheet 2 page in your workbook.

1. Click the **Sheet 2** tab at the bottom of the workbook to switch to that spreadsheet.
    Notice that there are no blank columns or rows in this list. That's a prerequisite for a successful sort. Now you'll perform an alphabetical sort.

2. Select any cell in **column A** that is within the list.

3. Choose **Home→Editing→Sort & Filter** ⬚ and then choose **Sort A to Z**.
    The list is now in alphabetical order by last name. Now you will perform a date sort.

4. Select any cell in **column C** that is within the list.

5. Choose **Home**→**Editing**→**Sort & Filter** and then choose **Sort Oldest to Newest**.

   The oldest date appears at the top of the list. Now you will perform a numeric sort.

6. Select any cell in **column E** that is within the list.

7. Choose **Home**→**Editing**→**Sort & Filter** and then choose **Sort Smallest to Largest**.

   The shifts are now in numeric order, starting with the first shift.

8. Save the file.

Working with Columns and Rows

Excel provides the ability to widen and narrow columns and rows, which means you can adjust them to fit the data you enter in them. Rows automatically adapt to the font size you use. You also have the ability to add and delete columns and rows.

Resizing Columns and Rows

If the data is too wide for a column, you can resize it so all of the data fits the column. If the data is narrow, you can narrow the column width.

When you position the mouse pointer on the border between the column headers, it changes to a double-headed arrow.

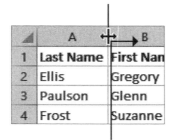

Pressing the mouse button and dragging to the right/left widens the column or makes it more narrow.

Positioning the mouse pointer on the border between two rows and dragging up/down widens the row or makes it more narrow.

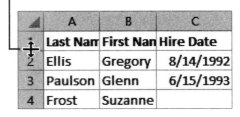

You can also double-click the border between two column or row headers. This makes the column or row wide or tall enough to accommodate the widest or tallest entry in the column. This is known as *Best Fit*.

HANDS-ON 5.11 Resize Columns

In this exercise, you will resize columns to accommodate the width of the column headings.

1. Position the mouse pointer on the border between **columns A** and **B**.

   The mouse pointer changes to a double-headed arrow.

   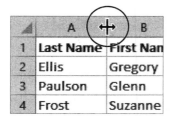

2. Press the mouse button and drag to the right.

3. Release the mouse button when you think *Last Name* is fully visible.

4. If you didn't make the column wide enough, repeat the process until you can see the entire column heading.

5. Position the mouse pointer on the border between **columns B** and **C**.

   The mouse pointer changes to a double-headed arrow.

6. Press the mouse button and then drag to the right to widen the column enough to see the complete column heading.

7. Position the mouse pointer between **columns D** and **E**.

8. When the pointer changes to a double-headed arrow, double-click to make the column wide enough for the column data.

9. Use the double-click technique to widen **columns F** and **G**.

10. Save the file.

· ·

Inserting and Deleting Columns and Rows

Once you create a spreadsheet, you may discover that you need to add or remove entire columns or rows. For example, you may need to accommodate a change in the data. You can add or delete a single column or row, or you can add or delete multiple columns or rows at once.

If you select multiple rows or columns before issuing the Insert or Delete command (as described in the table on the next page), the same number of rows or columns that you select will be inserted or deleted.

Note! Undo works as well in Excel as it does in Word.

QUICK REFERENCE: Inserting and Deleting Columns and Rows

Task	Procedure
Insert rows	■ Select the row where you want the new row to appear. ■ Choose Home→Cells→Insert menu button ▾→ Insert Sheet Rows.
Insert columns	■ Select the column where you want the new column to appear. ■ Choose Home→Cells→Insert menu button ▾→ Insert Sheet Columns.
Delete rows	■ Select the row to delete. ■ Choose Home→Cells→Delete menu button ▾→ Delete Sheet Rows.
Delete columns	■ Select the column to delete. ■ Choose Home→Cells→Delete menu button ▾→ Delete Sheet Columns.

HANDS-ON 5.12 Insert and Delete Columns and Rows

In this exercise, you will insert and delete columns and rows in your Training Roster file. A firefighter just transferred from another station in your county. He was hired in 1995. Rather than adding him at the bottom of the list and re-sorting the data, you'll add his record above row 4.

1. Position the mouse pointer on the row header for **row 4** and then click to select the row.

	A	B	C	D
1	**Last Name**	**First Name**	**Hire Date**	**Rank**
2	Ellis	Gregory	8/14/1992	Firefighter/EMT-Intermediate
3	Paulson	Glenn	6/15/1993	Firefighter
4	Frost	Suzanne	5/19/1996	Firefighter/EMT-Basic
5	Morgan	Jack	8/1/1996	Firefighter
6	Sanchez	Barbara	9/1/1997	Firefighter/EMT-Paramedic

2. Choose **Home→Cells→Insert ▦ menu button ▾** and then choose **Insert Sheet Rows**.

   Row 4 is now a blank row.

3. Type the information shown in row 4:

	A	B	C	D	E	F	G
1	Last Name	First Name	Hire Date	Rank	Shift	Training	Completed
2	Ellis	Gregory	8/14/1992	Firefighter/EMT-Intermediate	1	EMT-Paramedic	x
3	Paulson	Glenn	6/15/1993	Firefighter	1	Additional Fire	
4	Malik	Hasan	12/4/1995	Firefighter	1	Additional Fire	

Some firefighters are involved in community outreach programs. As part of the database, the chief wants to track which programs the firefighters are involved in. Now you will add a new column for outreach tracking between columns D and E.

4. Position the mouse pointer at the top of **column E**.

5. When the mouse pointer changes to a down-pointing arrow, click to select the column.

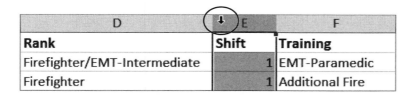

D	E	F
Rank	Shift	Training
Firefighter/EMT-Intermediate	1	EMT-Paramedic
Firefighter	1	Additional Fire

6. Choose **Home→Cells→Insert** ⊞ **menu button** ▾ and then choose **Insert Sheet Columns**.

After showing the database to the chief, he says he would rather have the Community Outreach column as the last column, so you will now delete the column you just added.

7. If necessary, position the mouse pointer on the column header for **column E** and click to select the column.

8. Choose **Home→Cells→Delete** ⊞ **menu button** ▾ and then choose **Delete Sheet Columns**.

Next you will type the new column heading in cell H1.

9. Click **cell H1**, type `Community Outreach`, and tap Enter.

Now you need to widen the column to accommodate the long heading.

10. Position the mouse pointer on the border between **columns H** and **I**.

11. When the mouse pointer changes to a double-headed arrow, double-click to widen **column H**.

12. Save and close the file.

Self-Assessment

Check your knowledge of this chapter's key concepts and skills by completing the Self-Assessment.

Page number

1. When you navigate with scroll bars, the active cell does not move.   **true false** _____

2. When you're in the process of entering data in a spreadsheet, the **true false** _____ Cancel and Enter buttons appear more bold on the Formula Bar.

3. Only the cells in columns A through Z have addresses.   **true false** _____

4. Excel's Sort feature allows you to sort numbers but not dates.   **true false** _____

5. If you want to sort a list, you should not have any blank columns **true false** _____ or rows in the list.

6. By default, Excel aligns numbers to the left edge of the cell.   **true false** _____

7. What are the three kinds of entries in spreadsheets?

   A. Formulas, text, and numbers

   B. Formulas, numbers, and the Ribbon

   C. Numbers, text, and cells

   D. Numbers, formulas, and columns

   Page number: _____

8. Use the Freeze Panes feature when _____.

   A. you don't want the data to be modified

   B. you want to keep column headings visible while scrolling down

   C. you want to select a cell range

   D. you want to copy data

   Page number: _____

9. You may want to add columns or rows to a spreadsheet because _____.

   A. there aren't typically enough cells in an Excel spreadsheet

   B. you have to add new columns and rows before you can sort data

   C. you must add new columns and rows before you can freeze panes

   D. you need to accommodate a change in the data

   Page number: _____

10. Which of the following is NOT true about cell ranges?

   A. A range of cells is a group of adjacent cells.

   B. You must select a range of cells before moving or copying them.

   C. When you select a range of cells, the active cell appears in the center of the range.

   D. Cell ranges are identified by the cell addresses in the upper-left and lower-right corners of the range.

   Page number: _____

Skill Builders

Enter Data and Work with Columns and Rows

In this exercise, you will review techniques for entering data in a spreadsheet. You will also use this opportunity to change the width of a column and to delete a column and a row. You are keeping a list of places your friends might like to see when they visit you, and you would like to add some more places of interest to your list. Remember, entering data is a two-step process.

1. Open **sb-Tourist Attractions** from your **Chapter 05** folder.

2. Select **cell A17**, type **Blues Festival**, and tap → twice to finish entering the data and move to **column C**.
   Cell C17 is now the active cell.

3. Type **Fort Mason** and tap → to finish entering the data.
   Cell D17 is now the active cell.

4. Type **September** and tap Enter to finish entering the data.

5. Tap Home to change the active cell to **cell A18**.

6. Type **Grand National Rodeo** and tap → twice to move to **cell C18**.

7. Type **Cow Palace** and then tap Tab to enter the data and move to **cell D18**.

8. Type **October-November** in **cell D18** and tap Enter to complete the entry.
   The data in column A is flowing into column B. You will adjust column A to accommodate the data.

9. Position the mouse pointer between **columns A** and **B**.

10. When the mouse pointer changes to a double-headed arrow, drag to the right until the vertical line is to the right of the longest entry; release the mouse button.

Delete a Column and a Row
You no longer need column B, and you would also like to delete the blank row 2.

11. Position the mouse pointer on the column header for **column B**.

12. When the mouse pointer changes to a down-pointing arrow, click to select the column.

13. Choose **Home→Cells→Delete ▧ menu button ▾** and then choose **Delete Sheet Columns**.

14. Position the mouse pointer on the row header for **row 2**.

15. When the mouse pointer changes to a right-pointing arrow, click to select the row.

16. Choose **Home→Cells→Delete menu button** ▾ and then choose **Delete Sheet Rows**.

17. Save and close the file.

··

SKILL BUILDER 5.2 Navigate, Freeze Panes, and Sort Data

In this exercise, you will move around a spreadsheet, freeze panes, and sort data. Your boss has asked to see the data represented in a few different ways, and Excel's Freeze Panes and Sort features make preparing data for your boss's review a simple matter.

1. Open **sb-Employee Roster** from your **Chapter 05** folder.

2. Click the **scroll down** ▾ button at the bottom of the scroll bar three times to place **row 4** at the top of the spreadsheet.

3. Click the **scroll up** ▴ button at the top of the scroll bar three times to place **row 1** at the top of the spreadsheet.

4. Click the open part of the **scroll bar** below the scroll box to move down one screen.

5. Press Ctrl + Home to move to **cell A1**.

6. Press Ctrl + End to move to the end of the data in the spreadsheet.

7. Tap Home to move to the beginning of the row.

8. Click **cell C2**.

9. Choose **View→Window→Freeze Panes** and then choose **Freeze Panes**.

10. Scroll down and notice that you can still see the column headings.

11. Scroll to the right until **column F** is next to **column B**.

Unfreeze Panes and Sort Data

12. Choose **View→Window→Freeze Panes** and then choose **Unfreeze Panes**.

13. Click anywhere in **column I** within the list.

14. Choose **Home→Editing→Sort & Filter** and then choose **Sort A to Z**.
    The list is now in alphabetical order by department. Next you will sort by zip code.

15. Click anywhere in **column G** within the list.

16. Choose **Home**→**Editing**→**Sort & Filter** [icon] and then choose **Sort Smallest to Largest**.

    Finally, you will sort by last name.

17. Select **cell A2**.

18. Choose **Home**→**Editing**→**Sort & Filter** [icon] and then choose **Sort A to Z**.

19. Save and close the file.

· ·

SKILL BUILDER 5.3 **Select Ranges, Edit, and Copy Data**

In this exercise, you will make editing changes and copy data from one spreadsheet to three other spreadsheets. Your manager asked you to set up an Expenses and Revenues report she can use to track all four regions she is responsible for. The ability to copy data makes this an easy task.

1. Open **sb-Expenses and Revenues by Region** from your **Chapter 05** folder.

    Under Expenses, the Rent category should really be Rent/Utilities, *so you will make that change first. Then you will add an Advertising category to Expenses.*

2. Select **cell B5** and notice the contents of **cell B5** in the Formula Bar.

3. Click in the **Formula Bar** following the word *Rent,* type **/Utilities**, and tap [Enter].

    Now you'll insert a blank row above row 6 for the Advertising expense category.

4. Position the mouse pointer on the **row 6 header**.

5. When the mouse pointer changes to a right-pointing arrow, click to select the row.

6. Choose **Home**→**Cells**→**Insert** [icon] **menu button** ▾ and then choose **Insert Sheet Rows**.

7. Select **cell B6**, type **Advertising**, and then tap [Enter].

Copy Data from One Spreadsheet to Another

You've already set up spreadsheet tabs for the South, East, and West Regions. Since all four regions have the same expense and revenue items, you can just copy the data from the North Region into the other spreadsheets.

8. Select **cell B2** and then hold down [Shift] and click **cell D16** to select a range of cells.

9. Choose **Home**→**Clipboard**→**Copy** [icon].

10. Click the **South Region** tab to switch to that spreadsheet and then select **cell B2**.

11. Choose **Home→Clipboard→Paste** [icon].

    The data was copied, but notice that the column widths are different from the original. Next you will use the Excel smart tag to keep the column widths the same as those for the North Region.

12. Follow these steps to keep the original column widths:

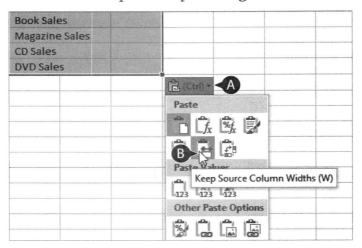

   Ⓐ Click the **smart tag** to display its menu.

   Ⓑ Choose the second icon in the second row, **Keep Source Column Widths**.

   The column widths now match those used for the North Region.

13. Click the **North Region** tab and notice that the flashing marquee is still active, indicating that the copied material is still in the Clipboard. You don't have to copy it again.

Copy the Data to the East and West Regions

14. Click the **East Region** tab to switch to that spreadsheet and then select **cell B2**.

15. Choose **Home→Clipboard→Paste** [icon].

16. Click the **smart tag** at the bottom-right corner of the pasted data and choose the second icon in the second row, **Keep Source Column Widths**.

    You can now go straight to the West Region tab since the copied information is still in the Clipboard.

17. Click the **West Region** tab and select **cell B2**.

18. Choose **Home→Clipboard→Paste** [icon].

19. Use the **smart tag** to maintain the column widths from the source data.

20. Switch back to the **South Region** tab and correct the region name in **cell D2**.

21. Now correct the East and West Region names.

22. Save and close the file.

23. Exit Excel.

Budgeting with Calculations and Charts

In this chapter, you will dive into calculations, one of Excel's most useful features. Like a calculator, Excel can add, subtract, multiply, and divide. You will also build eye-catching column and pie charts that summarize data and reveal numeric trends. Picturing your data in charts makes it easy to understand that data at a glance.

LEARNING OBJECTIVES

- Use Excel's mathematical operators
- Build formulas
- Perform calculations using Excel's built-in functions
- Copy formulas and functions
- Create charts to visualize your data

📂 Project: Tracking Inventory Expenses

Ken Turner owns a marine supply store on the San Francisco Bay. He carefully tracks his inventory costs to make sure he keeps his expenses in line.

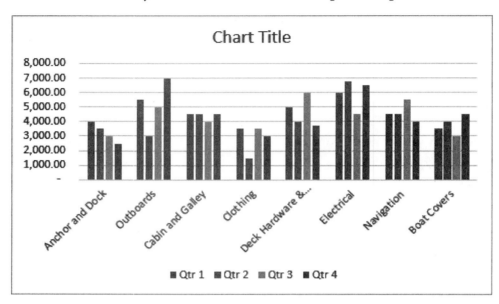

Ken's year-end inventory analysis shows that his inventory expenses have remained pretty steady throughout the year.

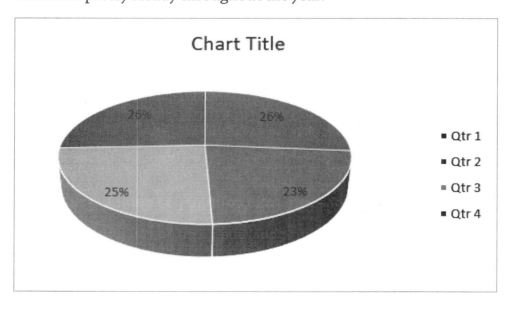

What Is a Formula?

Does the word *formula* make you hyperventilate? If the answer is yes, you may be one of those unfortunate people who had an unpleasant introduction to math. Did you know that 2+2 is a formula? Okay, now you can relax.

Just because you use a spreadsheet to perform calculations, it doesn't mean you will suddenly use some strange branch of mathematics. You're going to use the kind of math you have always used; you're just going to do it electronically.

Excel's Mathematical Operators

There are a few slight differences in performing calculations electronically versus on paper, but they are not difficult to understand. You are no doubt familiar with the signs used for addition, subtraction, multiplication, and division. If you look around on your keyboard for the multiplication and division signs you normally use, you won't find them, and because of this, in Excel you use the forward slash (/) for the division sign and the asterisk (*) for the multiplication sign.

MATHEMATICAL OPERATORS IN EXCEL

Operation	Symbol
Add	+
Subtract	-
Multiply	*
Divide	/

An easy way to remember the operators is to look at the number pad (if your computer has one) on the right side of the keyboard. You can use the keys shown in the following illustration when you create formulas. There are also duplicates of these keys on the main part of the keyboard. You can use whichever keys you prefer—or even a combination of them—as they work the same way.

How to Type a Formula

You need to take a slightly different approach when creating electronic formulas than you do when jotting down a formula on a notepad. For example, the placement of the equals (=) sign is different from what you might expect, and in addition to using numbers in formulas, you can use cell addresses, which is typically the preferred method.

Where's the Equals Sign?

In Excel, you use the same equals (=) sign you've always used; it's just that you place it at the beginning of the formula rather than at the end.

Instead of typing

    2+2=

You type

    =2+2

Why? When you enter data in a spreadsheet, your computer is watching to see what kind of data it is. If the first thing it sees is a number or an alphabetic character, it assumes that standard data is coming down the line and that it doesn't have to do anything complex. If your computer sees an equals (=) sign first, it figures, "Hey, this is a formula. I'd better pay attention because I have some work to do. I have to figure out the answer to this formula."

Numbers or Cell Addresses?

You can create formulas using numbers as in the preceding =2+2 example; however, most of the time you should use cell addresses, such as =A1+A2. The reason for this is that if you use numbers in a formula and later decide to change one of those numbers in the spreadsheet, the formula *will not recalculate*. If you use cell addresses, the formula *will recalculate*.

HANDS-ON 6.1 Enter Formulas in a Spreadsheet

In this exercise, you will create formulas in a budget spreadsheet using two techniques. You will begin by calculating the Qtr 1 Budget Total for Other Expenses. Later you will total the entire column, but for now you will just use the four numbers in Other Expenses to keep the task simple.

1. If necessary, start Excel.

2. Open **Pacific Marine Expense Budget** from your **Chapter 06** folder.

3. Take a moment to look over the spreadsheet and then select **cell B17**.
   Always start a formula by selecting the cell that will contain the answer.

Tip! When you type cell addresses in a formula, you can use uppercase or lowercase letters, as Excel will automatically convert lowercase addresses to uppercase.

4. Type the formula **=B13+B14+B15+B16** and then tap Enter.
   The answer 6,200.00 appears in cell B17.

5. Select **cell B17** and look at the Formula Bar.
   While the answer appears in cell B17, the formula behind the answer appears in the Formula Bar. This makes it easy to double-check your formulas for accuracy.

f_x	=B13+B14+B15+B16

   Now you'll try another formula, but this time you'll use the mouse to help you select cells. You will calculate the Qtr 1 Actual Total for Other Expenses. Again, you are just using four numbers for now to keep it simple.

6. Follow these steps to create a formula using the mouse:

12	Other Expenses		
13	Rent	4,500.00	4,500.00 **B**
14	Office Supplies	600.00 **C**	650.00
15	Advertising	600.00	450.00 **D**
16	Miscellaneous	500.00 **E**	300.00
17	Total	6,200 **A**	=C13
18			

A Select **cell C17** and type an equals (**=**) sign to begin the formula.

B Click **cell C13** and notice that *C13* appears in the formula. Type a plus (**+**) sign.

C Click **cell C14** and notice that this cell address is added to the formula. Type a plus (**+**) sign.

D Click **cell C15** and type a plus (**+**) sign.

E Click **cell C16** and tap ⌐Enter⌐ to finish the formula.

Using the mouse to help you create formulas is easy and reduces the likelihood that you will make a typo.

7. Select **cell C17** and look at the Formula Bar.

The answer appears in cell C17, and the formula appears in the Formula Bar.

Edit a Number That Appears in a Formula

You just discovered that the Actual figure for Miscellaneous expenses should be $400.00 instead of $300.00. Bear in mind that the current answer in cell C17 is $5,900.00.

8. Select **cell C16**, type **400**, and tap ⌐Enter⌐.

Look at the answer in cell C17 (6,000.00). The formula automatically recalculated. Remember, if you use cell addresses in formulas instead of numbers, the formulas recalculate automatically. In the next topic, you'll learn a slicker way to add a column of numbers that prevents you from having to enter formulas.

9. Click and drag to select **cells B17** and **C17**, then tap ⌐Delete⌐.

10. Save the file.

Always leave your file open unless directed otherwise.

Using Built-in Functions

There is another approach you can use to perform calculations. Excel has built-in functions that contain formulas that you don't have to write from scratch. These are real time-savers! Here are some of Excel's most popular functions.

COMMON EXCEL FUNCTIONS

Function	Description
=SUM(A1:A100)	Adds all numbers in the range A1 through A100
=MAX(A1:A100)	Finds the largest number in the range A1 through A100
=MIN(A1:A100)	Finds the smallest number in the range A1 through A100
=AVERAGE(A1:A100)	Finds the average for the numbers in the range A1 through A100

How Functions Are Constructed

Functions are built in a specific manner:

- Like formulas, functions begin with an equals (=) sign.

- Next to be inserted is the name of the function, such as SUM or AVERAGE.

- After that is a set of parentheses that usually contains one or more arguments. An *argument* is information necessary for a calculation. The range A1:A100 is the argument in each of the examples in the preceding table.

The Sum Button

Probably the most frequently used function is SUM; therefore, Excel provides the convenient Sum button on the Ribbon to automatically calculate sums for you.

Note! Depending on your screen's resolution, this button may be labeled AutoSum. The ToolTip labels the button as Sum, so the button will be described as the Sum button in this course.

 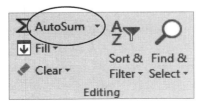

What Do the Pound Signs Mean?

When you have alphabetic or alphanumeric data that is too wide for a cell and there is data to the right of that cell, Excel visually chops off the text. In situations such as this, it's pretty obvious that the column is too narrow, and you can choose to widen it. When it comes to the answers to formulas, though, if Excel chops off part of the number, you may not realize it—and you might assume that what you see is correct. To prevent that possible confusion, Excel places pound signs in the cell as a warning that the column needs to be widened to see the entire number.

######
650.00
450.00
400.00
######

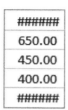 HANDS-ON 6.2 Use the SUM Function

In this exercise, you will use the SUM function to add a series of numbers in the Budget and Actual columns for the first quarter. First, you will manually type the function, and then you will use the Sum button to automatically enter the function. Finally, you will create a subtraction formula from scratch.

Note! Ignore the prompts that pop up when you type functions. You will not use them in this chapter.

1. Select **cell B17**.

2. Type the function **=SUM(B4:B16)** and then tap ⌷Enter⌷ to complete the function.

   Remember, in the last exercise you only added the four numbers in rows 13 through 16 to avoid typing lots of cell addresses. With the convenient SUM function, you can easily indicate a range *of cell addresses rather than typing each cell address. This method is particularly convenient when adding a long row or column of numbers. Now you will use the Sum button to automatically create a formula.*

3. Select **cell C17**.

4. Choose **Home→Editing→Sum** Σ.

   The Sum feature adds a flashing marquee around cells C13 through C16. Sum only went up to C13 because of the blank cell in C12. This isn't correct; you want to add the entire column, C4:C16. No problem; you can easily override Sum's decision.

5. Follow these steps to total the entire column:

Actual	Difference
4,000.00	
5,500.00	
4,500.00	
3,500.00	
5,000.00	
6,000.00	
4,500.00	
3,500.00	
4,500.00	
650.00	
450.00	
300.00	
=SUM(C13:C16)	
SUM(**number1**, [numbe	

A Place the mouse pointer on the square in the upper-right corner of the box around the **range C13:C16**. The pointer changes to a double-headed arrow.

B Click and drag up to the top of **cell C4** to place the box around the entire column of numbers; release the mouse button.

The formula is now =SUM(C4:C16).

6. Tap ⌷Enter⌷ to complete the formula.

Excel places pound signs in the cell. That's because the answer to the formula is too wide to fit in the cell.

7. Position the mouse pointer on the border between the column headers for **columns C** and **D**. When the mouse pointer changes to a double-headed arrow, double-click to adjust the column width.

Note! Continue to use this technique when you need to widen columns throughout this chapter.

Here's another technique to make sure Sum adds the numbers you want it to.

8. Click and drag to select the **range E4:E17**.

You're selecting the column of numbers you want to add plus a blank cell at the bottom of the column. This tells Excel to place the answer in the blank cell.

9. Choose **Home→Editing→Sum Σ**.

Excel places the answer in cell E17.

10. Click **cell E17** and check out the formula in the Formula Bar.

11. Widen **column E**.

12. Use the same technique to add the numbers in **column F** and then widen the column.

    You can also use that technique with multiple columns at the same time.

13. Select the **range H4:I17**.

14. Choose **Home→Editing→Sum** Σ.

    Excel placed answers in cells H17 and I17.

15. Check out the formulas in the Formula Bar and then widen the columns.

16. Use the same technique to add the numbers in **columns K** and **L** at the same time and then widen the columns.

Enter a Subtraction Formula

There is no built-in function for a simple subtraction problem, so you need to create this formula yourself—but you can get the mouse to give you a hand (paw).

17. Select **cell D4** and type an equals (=) sign.

18. Click **cell B4** and type a minus (–) sign.

19. Click **cell C4**, and then tap ⃞Enter to finish the formula.

20. Click **cell D4** and check the Formula Bar.

    The Actual Anchor and Dock inventory expense was $500.00 over budget; therefore, the answer is in parentheses to indicate a negative number.

    You don't have to retype this formula for all the numbers in columns B and C. Later you will learn to copy formulas—another big time-saver in Excel.

21. Select **cell G4** and type an equals (=) sign.

22. Click **cell E4** and type a minus (–) sign.

23. Click **cell F4** and then tap ⃞Enter to finish the formula.

24. Use the same technique to enter subtraction formulas in **cells J4** and **M4**.

    The parentheses in the answers indicate that you were over budget for Anchor and Dock supplies for the first three quarters and then under budget for the fourth quarter.

25. Save the file.

Calculate with AVERAGE, MAX, and MIN

The AVERAGE function calculates the average of a range of cells. The MAX function finds the largest number in a range, while MIN determines the smallest number in a range.

HANDS-ON 6.3 Use AVERAGE, MAX, and MIN

In this exercise, you will use the AVERAGE, MAX, and MIN functions to quickly analyze inventory data in your workbook.

1. Click the **Inventory Analysis** tab at the bottom of the workbook to switch to that spreadsheet.

   First you will calculate the average for the four quarters. Again, you will get the mouse to help you.

2. Select **cell F2** and type **=AVERAGE (**, but don't type the cell addresses.

3. Click and drag to select the **range B2:E2**.

   Notice that the range addresses automatically appear in the formula. You don't have to type the right (closed) parenthesis; Excel will do that for you.

4. Tap Enter .

5. Select **cell F2** and look at the Formula Bar.

   Now you can see that Excel put the right parenthesis in the formula for you.

6. Select **cell G2** and type **=MAX (** , but don't type the cell addresses.

7. Click and drag to select the **range B2:E2** and then tap Tab to finish the function and make **cell H2** active.

8. Type **=MIN (** in **cell H2**.

9. Click and drag to select the **range B2:E2** and then tap Enter .

   You're going to learn to copy formulas soon, so you won't have to create these formulas for every row.

10. Save the file.

Copying Formulas and Functions

You can copy formulas and functions because Excel automatically changes cell addresses in a copied formula *relative to* where it is copied. For example, if the

=SUM(A1:A100) function is copied one column to the right (column B), the function changes to *=SUM(B1:B100)*.

Here's another example: If you copy the function *=SUM(B9:H9)* down one row (row 10), the function changes to *=SUM(B10:H10)*. This is known as *relative referencing*, and it's one of the great powers of electronic spreadsheets. Without relative referencing, you would have to create formulas and functions one at a time.

You can use the same Copy button to copy formulas that you use to copy other types of data.

HANDS-ON 6.4 Copy Functions and Formulas

In this exercise, you will copy functions and formulas in both spreadsheets in your workbook. You will start with the *=AVERAGE* function in cell F2 of the Inventory Analysis worksheet.

1. Select **cell F2**.
2. Choose **Home→Clipboard→Copy** 🗐.
    Excel places a flashing marquee around the cell you are copying.
3. Select the **range F3:F9**.
4. Choose **Home→Clipboard→Paste** 📋.
5. Tap ⌷Esc⌷ to turn off the marquee.
6. Click **cell F2** and examine the formula; click **cell F3** and examine the formula.
    Notice that the range of cells inside the parentheses changed from B2:E2 to B3:E3. Excel changed the cell addresses relative to where the formula was copied. Now you will copy the MAX and MIN functions.
7. Select **cell G2**.
8. Choose **Home→Clipboard→Copy** 🗐 and then select the **range G3:G9**.
9. Choose **Home→Clipboard→Paste** 📋.
10. Select **cell H2**; copy the function and then paste it into **H3:H9**.
    Now you will calculate the inventory totals for all four quarters at once.
11. Select the **range B2:E10**.
12. Choose **Home→Editing→Sum** Σ.
    Excel places the total for each selected column in row 10.

Copy the Formulas in the Difference Columns

13. Click the **Expense Budget** tab at the bottom of the workbook to switch to that spreadsheet.

14. Select **cell D4**.

15. Choose **Home→Clipboard→Copy** 📑 and then select the **range D5:D16**.

    Note that you won't copy the formula to cell D17 since row 17 is labeled as a Total row. You are not totaling the Difference column; you are copying the subtraction formula.

16. Choose **Home→Clipboard→Paste** 📋.

    Take a moment to examine a couple of copied formulas and notice that the cell addresses changed in a relative fashion.

    Row 12 should be blank, so now you will delete the formula in cell D12.

17. Select **cell D12** and tap ⌈Delete⌋.

18. Use the same technique to copy the Difference formulas in **columns G**, **J**, and **M** and then delete **cells G12**, **J12**, and **M12**.

19. Save the file.

· ·

Using Charts to Visualize Data

Excel's charting features make charting data easy, and the results are stunning. Depicting your data with charts allows you to easily see trends and make comparisons in your data.

Excel offers a variety of chart types. Two of the most common are column and pie charts. Column charts compare categories of data using vertical columns. Each column represents values from a data series in the spreadsheet. Pie charts are round (like pies) and are used for comparing parts (slices) of the whole (pie).

Which Cells Do I Select?

To create a chart, you start by selecting the data you want to represent. Knowing which cells to select prior to creating the chart is important.

Column Charts

Column charts compare values across categories. For a column chart, you select the data but typically not a total row or total column. The following data selection allows you to compare the various Inventory categories to each other by quarter, but it does not include the totals from row 10.

▲	A	B	C	D	E	F
1	Actual Inventory Expense	Qtr 1	Qtr 2	Qtr 3	Qtr 4	Avg of Qtrs
2	Anchor and Dock	4,000.00	3,500.00	3,000.00	2,500.00	3,250.00
3	Outboards	5,500.00	3,000.00	5,000.00	7,000.00	5,125.00
4	Cabin and Galley	4,500.00	4,500.00	4,000.00	4,500.00	4,375.00
5	Clothing	3,500.00	1,500.00	3,500.00	3,000.00	2,875.00
6	Deck Hardware & Fastener	5,000.00	4,000.00	6,000.00	3,750.00	4,687.50
7	Electrical	6,000.00	6,750.00	4,500.00	6,500.00	5,937.50
8	Navigation	4,500.00	4,500.00	5,500.00	4,000.00	4,625.00
9	Boat Covers	3,500.00	4,000.00	3,000.00	4,500.00	
10	Total	36,500.00	31,750.00	34,500.00	35,750.00	

The following chart was created from the data selected in the previous illustration. It compares the inventory categories across four quarters. For example, you can see that Qtr 1 had the highest inventory cost for Anchor and Dock supplies, while Qtr 4 had the highest inventory cost for Outboards.

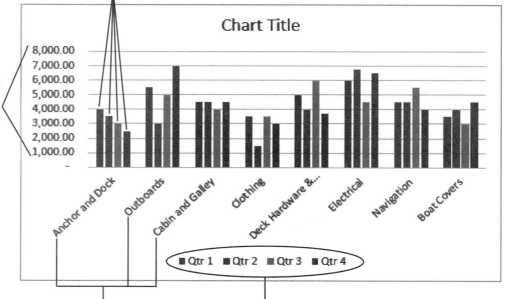

Columns represent values from the various data series. The first data series is the Quarter 1 numbers in column B. The first column in each inventory category represents the Quarter 1 data, the second column represents the Quarter 2 data, and so forth.

Excel created these labels after it determined the range of values included in the chart.

These labels (Anchor and Dock, Outboards, Cabin and Galley, etc.) come from column A of the selected cells.

This legend identifies the columns. The legend text (Qtr 1, Qtr 2, Qtr 3, Qtr 4) comes from the first row of selected cells.

Pie Charts

Pie charts compare pieces of the whole. You typically select two sets of data: the values to be represented by the slices of the pie (totals in row 10 in the following example) and the legend data needed to identify the slices (row 1 in the following example).

Tip! To select nonadjacent ranges of cells, select the first range and then press Ctrl while dragging over additional ranges.

Legend labels

	A	B	C	D	E
1	Actual Inventory Expense	Qtr 1	Qtr 2	Qtr 3	Qtr 4
2	Anchor and Dock	4,000.00	3,500.00	3,000.00	2,500.00
3	Outboards	5,500.00	3,000.00	5,000.00	7,000.00
4	Cabin and Galley	4,500.00	4,500.00	4,000.00	4,500.00
5	Clothing	3,500.00	1,500.00	3,500.00	3,000.00
6	Deck Hardware & Fastener	5,000.00	4,000.00	6,000.00	3,750.00
7	Electrical	6,000.00	6,750.00	4,500.00	6,500.00
8	Navigation	4,500.00	4,500.00	5,500.00	4,000.00
9	Boat Covers	3,500.00	4,000.00	3,000.00	4,500.00
10	Total	36,500.00	31,750.00	34,500.00	35,750.00

Values represented by the slices of the pie

This chart was created from the data selected in the previous illustration. The slices compare the total inventory expense for each of the four quarters. In this case, the inventory expenses for each quarter are almost equal.

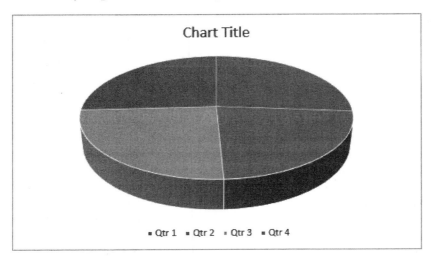

Chart Title

■ Qtr 1   ■ Qtr 2   ■ Qtr 3   ■ Qtr 4

Embedded Charts Compared to Chart Sheets

A chart can either be embedded with the data in the spreadsheet or placed on a separate sheet in the workbook. An embedded chart provides the benefit of making it easy to compare the data in the spreadsheet with the columns or slices in the chart. On the other hand, you may prefer to examine trends and comparisons without focusing on numeric details. A separate chart sheet works well for that and also makes it easy to print only the chart without the surrounding data.

HANDS-ON 6.5 Visualize Your Data with Charts

In this exercise, you will create two charts—a column chart and a pie chart—and you will create both an embedded chart and a chart sheet.

1. Click the **Inventory Analysis** tab and select the **range A1:E9**.

2. Choose **Insert→Charts→Insert Column or Bar Chart** 📊.
   The chart gallery opens, which allows you to choose various types of column charts.

3. Choose the first chart type in the 2-D Column category.

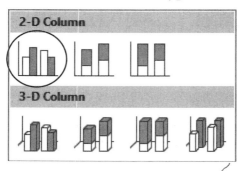

   The chart appears in the spreadsheet. The border surrounding the chart indicates it's selected. The chart must be selected if you want to make changes to it. Notice the contextual Chart Tools tabs (Design and Format) that appear on the Ribbon when the chart is selected.

4. Click in the spreadsheet to deselect the chart.
   The chart's surrounding border disappears, as well as the Chart Tools on the Ribbon.

5. Click the outer edge of the chart and the border reappears.
   Now you will move the embedded chart to its own chart sheet.

6. Choose **Chart Tools→Design→Location→Move Chart** 📊.
   The Move Chart dialog box appears. Here you can specify to move the chart to a New Sheet. The Object In *option in the dialog box refers to embedding a chart as an object in the spreadsheet, which is the option currently in effect.*

7. Choose **New Sheet** and then click **OK**.

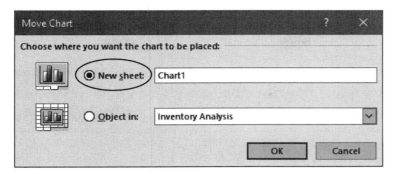

The chart now has its own sheet in the workbook. Notice the Chart 1 tab at the bottom of the workbook.

8. Click the **Inventory Analysis** tab to return to the inventory data.

   Notice that the embedded chart no longer appears in the spreadsheet.

Create a Pie Chart

Now you will select data from the Total row to be represented by pie slices. You will also select the column headings, which will appear in the legend. Remember that you can select multiple nonadjacent ranges by holding down Ctrl when selecting the second and subsequent ranges.

9. Select the **range B1:E1**.

10. Press Ctrl and select the **range B10:E10**; release the Ctrl key.

    The numbers in the range B10:E10 will determine the size of the slices. The entries in the range B1:E1 will become the entries in the legend, describing the meanings of the slices.

11. Choose **Insert→Charts→Insert Pie or Doughnut Chart** .

    The pie chart gallery appears.

12. Choose the chart type in the 3-D Pie category.

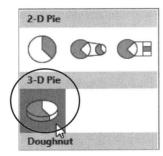

The pie chart now appears, embedded in the spreadsheet.

13. Save the file.

Moving and Resizing an Embedded Chart

You can move an embedded chart within a spreadsheet by dragging it with the mouse pointer when the pointer looks like a four-headed arrow. You can resize the chart when the mouse pointer looks like a double-headed arrow.

When the mouse pointer is on the border (but not on the circular resizing handles), it changes to the move pointer. You can then drag the chart to a new location.

You must select a chart before moving/resizing it. This border indicates that the chart is selected.

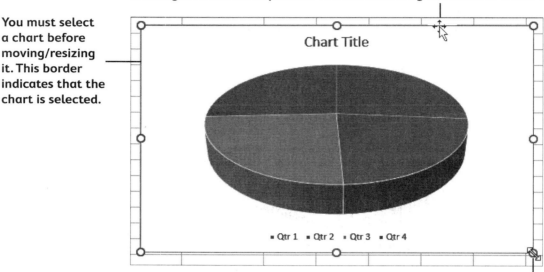

Placing the mouse pointer on the resizing handle changes it to this resizing pointer. You can then drag to change the size of the object. This process is similar to that used for resizing graphic objects in Word.

HANDS-ON 6.6 Move and Resize an Embedded Chart

In this exercise, you will move the embedded pie chart below the spreadsheet data. Then you will resize it.

1. If necessary, click the outer edge of the chart to select it.

2. Follow these steps to move the chart:

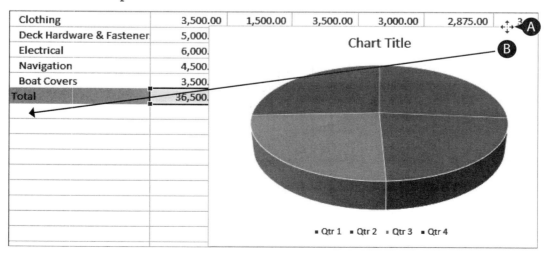

Ⓐ Place the mouse pointer on the chart border (but not on a resizing handle) and notice that it changes to a four-headed arrow.

Ⓑ Press and hold the mouse button, and drag the chart to position its upper-left corner as shown (in Column A and below the Total row). Release the mouse button.

Now you'll resize the chart.

3. Place the mouse pointer on the bottom-right resizing handle and notice that the pointer changes to a two-headed arrow.

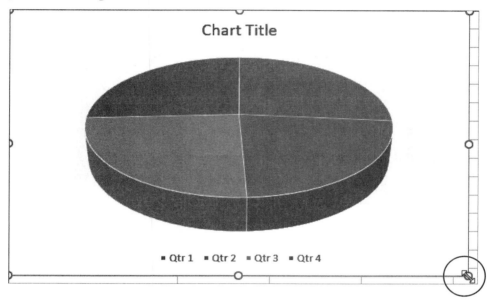

4. Drag up and to the left about half an inch to make the chart smaller.

5. Click in the spreadsheet to deselect the chart.

6. Save the file.

Design Tools

When you select a chart, two new Chart Tools tabs appear on the Ribbon: Design and Format. In this part of the chapter, you will spend some time working with the Design tab, which contains some appealing features for modifying your chart.

Switch Row/Column Data

Switching the row and column data in a column chart provides an interesting change of perspective on analyzing your data. This illustration displays the quarters as the legend and the inventory categories as the labels for the columns in the chart.

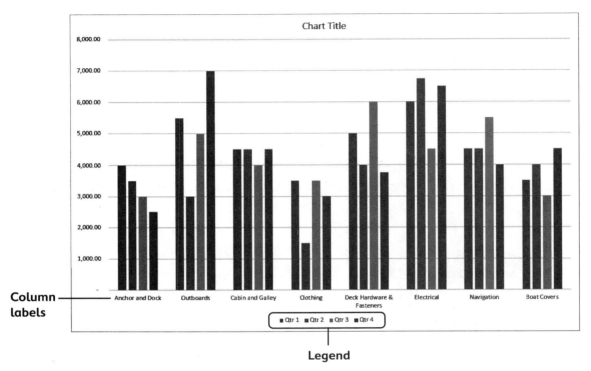

Switching the row and column data provides the following new perspective. Notice that the quarters now appear as column labels and the categories make up the legend.

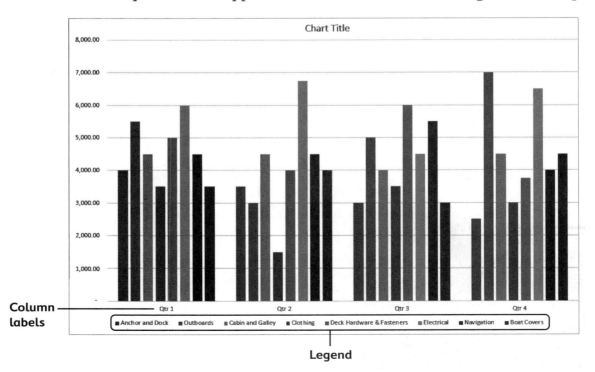

Chart Layouts

The Chart Layouts group on the Design tab provides various methods for labeling pieces of a chart, including numeric values and percentages of the whole.

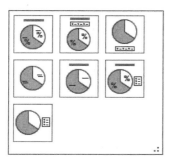

In this example, the chosen layout displays the slices of the pie as percentages of the whole. Excel has added a Chart Title object that you can modify with your own words.

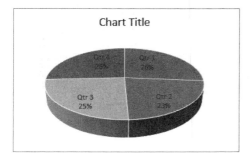

Chart Styles

The Chart Styles gallery offers attractive design and color combinations you can apply to your charts.

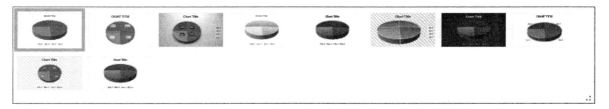

This dramatic change to the chart style was accomplished with a simple click of the mouse.

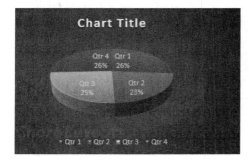

HANDS-ON 6.7 Modify the Chart Design

In this exercise, you will modify the design of charts by switching the row and column data, applying a new layout, and applying a new chart style.

1. Click the **Chart 1** tab at the bottom of the workbook to display the column chart.

   Observe the labels at the bottom of the columns and the legend below that. They will switch places when you switch the row and column data.

2. Click the border of the chart to select it.

3. Choose **Chart Tools→Design→Data→Switch Row/Column** 🔲.

   Observe the changes to the chart. The quarters appear at the bottom of the columns and the legend is below them. Now you will change a chart layout.

4. Click the **Inventory Analysis** tab at the bottom of the workbook to return to the pie chart.

5. If necessary, click the outer edge of the chart to select it.

6. Choose **Chart Tools→Design→Chart Layouts→Quick Layout** 🔳 to display various layouts.

7. Choose **Layout 6**.

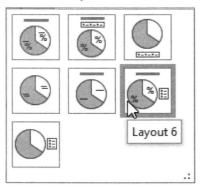

8. Follow these steps to observe the changes to the chart:

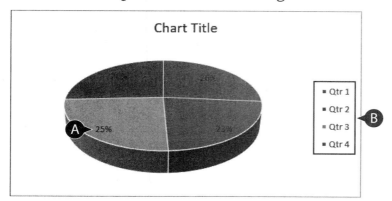

Ⓐ Notice that Excel displays the percent of the total for each slice of the pie.

Ⓑ Notice that the legend moved from the bottom of the chart to the right of the chart.

Now you will type a new chart title.

9. Click the **Chart Title** object to select it.

10. Type **Yearly Inventory Expense** as the new chart title; the title appears in the Formula Bar as you type.

11. Tap Enter.

Change the Chart Style

12. Choose **Chart Tools→Design→Chart Styles**.

13. Click the **More** button at the right edge of the Chart Styles gallery to display the entire gallery.

14. Choose **Style 3**.

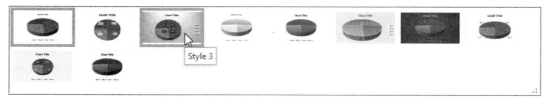

Tip!   Use ToolTips to assist you if necessary.

The chart now has a dramatic new look.

15. Save and close the file.

Self-Assessment

Check your knowledge of this chapter's key concepts and skills by completing the Self-Assessment.

Page number

1. Using charts allows you to easily see trends and make comparisons about your data. **true false** _____

2. All formulas begin with an equals (=) sign. **true false** _____

3. The multiplication symbol used in Excel is *x*. **true false** _____

4. Excel automatically changes the cell addresses in a copied formula relative to where it's copied. **true false** _____

5. If you want formulas to recalculate when a number changes, use numbers and not cell addresses. **true false** _____

6. An Excel chart can be embedded in a spreadsheet or appear on a separate chart sheet. **true false** _____

7. Which of these is NOT a built-in Excel function?

   A. MAX

   B. SUBTRACT

   C. AVERAGE

   D. SUM

   Page number: _____

8. Which of these is a mathematical operator in Excel?

   A. ?

   B. /

   C. &

   D. #

   Page number: _____

9. Which of these are Excel chart types?

   A. Pie and column

   B. Pie and Budget

   C. Medical and Column

   D. Medical and Pie

   Page number: _____

10. Why do Excel formulas begin with an equals sign?

   A. It's easier to type the equals sign at the beginning of the formula than at the end.

   B. Excel uses a different branch of mathematics than what you learned in school.

   C. It indicates to Excel that the data is a formula.

   D. It's the only key on the keyboard not reserved for other purposes.

   Page number: _____

 # Skill Builders

SKILL BUILDER 6.1 **Track the Men's Championship Golf Tournament**

In this exercise, you will use some of Excel's built-in functions. You are in charge of keeping track of the golf scores for the men's championship. It's the perfect opportunity for you to get more experience with entering and copying functions.

1. Open **sb-Golf Scores** from your **Chapter 06** folder.

2. Enter the data as shown for **rows 6–11**:

	A	B	C	D	E	F	G	H	I
1	Golf Week Men's Championship								
2									
3									
4									
5	Name	Day 1	Day 2	Day 3	Day 4	Tournament Total	Tournament Avg	Tournament Max	Tournament Min
6	Mukesh Patel	70	66	67	68				
7	Roger Kashner	72	68	69	71				
8	Moses LeVan	71	70	73	73				
9	Jose Menendez	70	69	76	75				
10	Albert Schultz	73	71	71	76				
11	Arnold Alvarez	69	75	75	72				

Now you'll use the SUM function to calculate the tournament total for each player.

3. Select **cell F6**.

4. Choose **Home→Editing→Sum Σ**.

   Excel places a marquee around Mukesh Patel's scores for the four days of the tournament.

5. Click the **Enter** ✔ button on the Formula Bar to finish entering the function.

   Now you will copy the function down so it can be used for the rest of the players. Cell F6 should still be active.

6. Choose **Home→Clipboard→Copy** 📋 and then select the **range F7:F11**.

7. Choose **Home→Clipboard→Paste** 📋.

8. Tap Esc to remove the flashing marquee.

   Mukesh Patel is our winner! He has the lowest score for the four-day tournament. Next you will calculate Mukesh's average score.

Use the AVERAGE, MAX, and MIN Functions

9. Select **cell G6** and type: **=AVERAGE (**

10. Select the **range B6:E6** and tap ⌷Tab⌷ to complete the formula.

    Now you will calculate Mukesh's maximum and minimum scores.

11. With **cell H6** as the active cell, type: **=MAX (**

12. Select the **range B6:E6** and tap ⌷Tab⌷ to finish entering the formula.

13. With **cell I6** as the active cell, type: **=MIN (**

14. Select the **range B6:E6** and tap ⌷Enter⌷.

    Now you will copy all three functions to the rest of the players at the same time.

15. Select the **range G6:I6**.

16. Choose **Home→Clipboard→Copy** 📋 and then select the **range G7:I11**.

17. Choose **Home→Clipboard→Paste** 📋.

    Now you see the average, maximum, and minimum scores for all of the players.

18. Tap ⌷Esc⌷ to turn off the marquee.

19. Save and close the file.

SKILL BUILDER 6.2 Calculate Nutrients and Chart the Data

Your doctor is concerned about your fondness for junk food. She wants you to have more calcium, protein, and fiber (and less cholesterol and saturated fats) in your diet. In this exercise, you will examine the nutritional value of various foods and use a chart to depict the data.

1. Open **sb-Counting Nutrients** from the **Chapter 06** folder.

    You will use the MAX and MIN functions to determine which foods are the highest and lowest in various nutrient categories.

2. Select **cell C12** and type: **=MAX (**

3. Select the **range C5:C10** and tap ⌷Enter⌷.

4. Type **=MIN (** in **cell C13**.

5. Select the **range C5:C10** and tap ⌷Enter⌷.

    Now you will copy the formulas.

6. Select the **range C12:C13**.

7. Choose **Home**→**Clipboard**→**Copy** 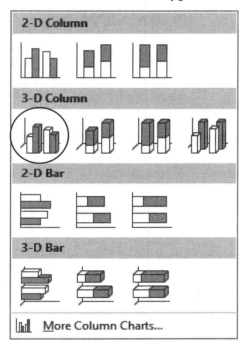 and then select the **range D12:G13**.

8. Choose **Home**→**Clipboard**→**Paste** .

9. Tap Esc to turn off the marquee.

   Now you see the maximum and minimum values for each nutrient category.

Chart the Nutrients

10. Select the **range B4:G10**.

11. Choose **Insert**→**Charts**→**Insert Column or Bar Chart** .

12. Choose the first chart type in the 3-D category.

Notice which of the foods are high and low in the various nutrient categories. Broccoli wins in the Calcium category.

13. Drag the chart below the data and position it where you think it looks best.

14. Click in the spreadsheet to deselect the chart.

15. Save and close the file.

SKILL BUILDER 6.3 Create a Household Budget

In this exercise, you will use your Excel skills to add formulas to your household budget. First you will compute the total monthly income and then you will find the total for all expense categories. Finally, you will subtract total expenses from total income to determine if you are over or under budget for the month.

1. Open **sb-Household Budget** from the **Chapter 06** folder.

2. Select **cell C8**.

3. Choose **Home→Editing→Sum** Σ and then tap Enter to complete the formula.

   This is your total monthly income. Let's hope it's enough to cover the expenses.

4. Select **cell C14**.

5. Choose **Home→Editing→Sum** Σ and then tap Enter to complete the formula.

6. Use the **Sum** Σ button to enter the totals for the remaining expense categories in **cells C22**, **C30**, and **C35**.

   Next you will compute the Total Expenses for January.

Create Formulas from Scratch

7. Select **cell C38** and use the mouse to help you create this formula:
   =C14+C22+C30+C35

8. Tap Enter to complete the formula.

   Now you will determine whether you are under or over budget.

9. With **cell C39** active, enter the formula **=C8−C38** and tap Enter.

   Congratulations! You are well under budget for the month.

10. Save and close the file.

SKILL BUILDER 6.4 Track Your Stocks

In this exercise, you will track a stock you are thinking about investing in. You want to examine its performance over time to see how it's doing.

1. Open **sb-Stock Tracker** from your **Chapter 06** folder.

   Seven weeks ago the XYZ stock closed at 36. You want to see how you would have fared if you had purchased 100 shares of the stock, so you start by calculating the total purchase price by multiplying the original price per share by the number of shares owned.

2. Select **cell E4** and type the formula =C4*D4.

3. Click the **Enter** ✔ button on the Formula Bar.

4. Copy the formula in **cell E4** down through **cell E9**.

5. Use this information to enter end-of-week prices in the **range B4:B9**:

Week 1	38
Week 2	39
Week 3	42
Week 4	35
Week 5	37
Week 6	39

   Now you will calculate the value for each week by multiplying the end-of-week price by the number of shares.

6. Select **cell F4** and type the formula =B4*D4.

7. Click the **Enter** ✔ button to complete the formula.

8. Copy the formula in **cell F4** down through **cell F9**.

   Now you will calculate the value for each week by multiplying the end-of-week price by the number of shares.

9. Click **cell G4**, type the formula =F4-E4, and click **Enter** ✔.

10. Copy the formula in **cell G4** down through **cell G9**.

11. Tap Esc to turn off the marquee.

Chart Your Data

12. Select the **range F3:G9**.

13. Choose **Insert→Charts→Insert Column or Bar Chart** 📊.

14. Choose the first chart type in the 3-D Column category.

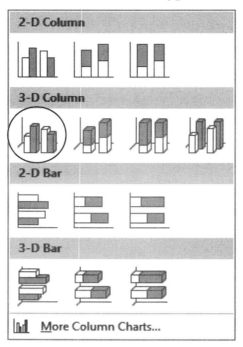

15. Drag the chart below the data.

16. Click in the spreadsheet to deselect the chart.

17. Save and close the file.

. . . .

SKILL BUILDER 6.5 Graph a Giraffe

In this exercise, you will create a giraffe graph. You are pursuing a degree in animal care and technology, and you think it would be interesting to track the heights of giraffes at your local zoo. The zookeeper has provided you with the height of each of their giraffes.

1. Open **sb-Giraffe Heights** from the **Chapter 06** folder.
   There are nine giraffes at the zoo: two adult males, three adult females, two yearlings, and two babies.

2. Select the **range A3:D6** and choose **Insert→Charts→ Insert Column or Bar Chart** ⓘ.

3. Choose the first chart type in the 3-D Column category.
   Now you will move the chart to its own sheet.

4. With the chart selected, choose **Chart Tools→Design→Location→ Move Chart** ⓘ.

5. Choose the **New Sheet** option in the Move Chart dialog box and click **OK**.
   The chart now appears on its own page in the workbook.

6. Save and close the file.

7. Exit Excel.

Creating Powerful Presentations

PowerPoint is designed for creating electronic presentations. It provides a multitude of tools and features for producing professional, polished presentations. Whether you are presenting at an important business meeting or delivering the results of a research project, PowerPoint will make your audience sit up and pay attention.

LEARNING OBJECTIVES

- Identify key parts of the PowerPoint window
- Navigate through a presentation
- Work with design themes and slide layouts
- Explore the different PowerPoint views
- Add clip art, animations, and transitions

Project: Create an Email Presentation

Safia Salman is a time-management expert. She has been invited to give a presentation on the efficient use of email at Central College's Career Day next month. Knowing the impact of email, she wants to create a presentation that will give her audience the tools they need to get it under control. Safia's dynamic speaking abilities, coupled with PowerPoint's robust presentation features, such as the ability to add interest using clip art, are sure to win over the audience.

What Is PowerPoint?

PowerPoint 2016 is an intuitive, powerful presentation graphics program that enables you to create dynamic, multimedia presentations. You can deliver your presentation directly from your computer or by using an overhead video projection system.

PowerPoint lets you concentrate on the content of your presentation instead of focusing on design details. Using PowerPoint's built-in design themes, animations, and transitions, you can create highly effective, professional presentations. PowerPoint tools help you organize, develop, and deliver your presentation with precision, control, and creativity.

HANDS-ON 7.1 Start PowerPoint

In this exercise, you will start the PowerPoint program.

1. If necessary, start your computer.

2. Click the **Start** button in the bottom-left corner of the screen.

3. Scroll down the alphabetical list and click **PowerPoint 2016**.
   The PowerPoint program loads and the PowerPoint Start screen appears.

4. **Maximize** the PowerPoint window if it isn't already maximized.
   Always leave your file open unless directed otherwise.

The PowerPoint Start Screen

When PowerPoint starts, it displays a Start screen that offers a variety of templates from which to choose. A Blank Presentation option is also available. Use it to create a blank, unformatted presentation to which you can add graphics, colors, and special fonts.

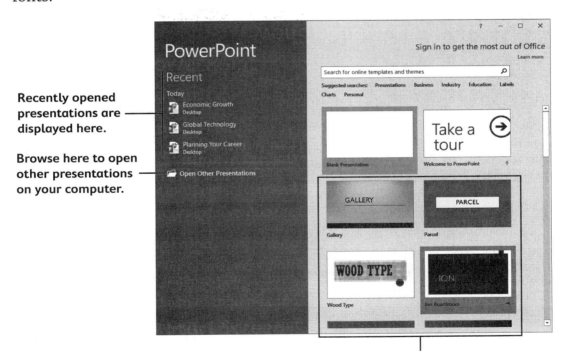

Recently opened presentations are displayed here.

Browse here to open other presentations on your computer.

You can choose a preformatted template on which to base your new presentation.

HANDS-ON 7.2 Create a Blank Presentation

In this exercise, you will create a new, blank presentation.

1. Click the **Blank Presentation** template on the PowerPoint Start screen.

   A new, blank presentation appears.

The PowerPoint Window

The PowerPoint program window, like most other Microsoft Office programs, groups commands on the Ribbon. This illustration provides an overview of the program window. Don't be concerned if your PowerPoint window looks slightly different from this example; just as in Word and Excel, the PowerPoint screen is customizable.

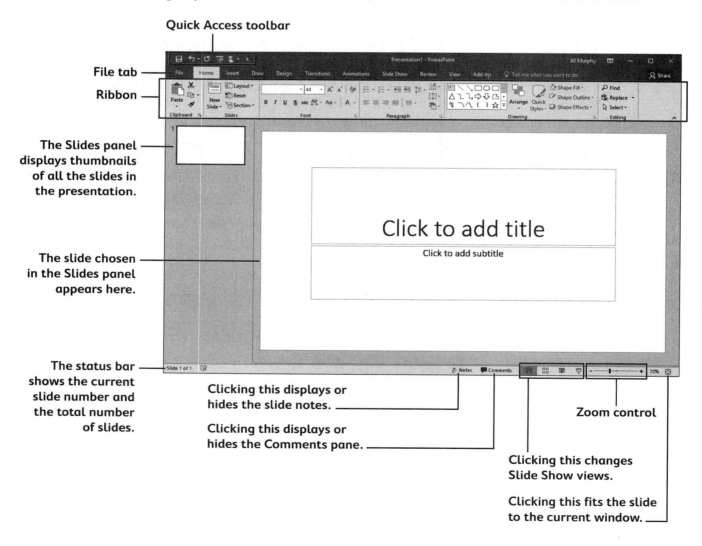

Navigating in a Presentation

PowerPoint has a number of both mouse and keyboard techniques for moving through a presentation. The technique you use is a matter of personal preference.

Dragging the scroll box moves through your slides. A ToolTip displays the slide's number and title to guide you as you scroll.

The Slides panel displays thumbnails of the presentation slides. Clicking a thumbnail icon switches to that slide in the main window.

The Previous Slide and Next Slide buttons allow you to move through the presentation one slide at a time.

QUICK REFERENCE: Navigating in PowerPoint

Task	Procedure
Move to the first slide	Drag the scroll box to the top of the scroll bar or press Ctrl + Home.
Move to the last slide	Drag the scroll box to the bottom of the scroll bar or press Ctrl + End.
Move to the next slide	Click Next Slide at the bottom of the scroll bar or tap Page Down.
Move to the previous slide	Click Previous Slide at the bottom of the scroll bar or tap Page Up.
Jump to a slide	Drag the scroll box and observe the ToolTip that displays the slide's number and title or click the desired thumbnail icon in the Slides panel.

🖱 HANDS-ON 7.3 Navigate in a Presentation

In this exercise, you will navigate through a presentation using different methods, including both mouse and keyboard techniques.

1. Choose **File→Close** and then choose **File→Open**, navigate to your **Chapter 07** folder, and open the **Time Management** presentation.

2. Click the **slide 2** thumbnail icon in the Slides panel to switch to that slide.

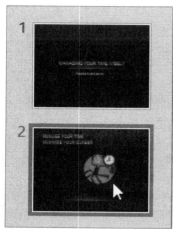

Slide 2 now appears in the main window.

3. Follow these steps to use the tools in the scroll bar to navigate:

Ⓐ Click the **Next Slide** button at the bottom of the scroll bar to move to slide 3.

Ⓑ Drag the **scroll box** to the bottom of the scroll bar to display the last slide in the presentation.

4. Press ⌈Ctrl⌉+⌈Home⌉ to move to the beginning of the presentation.

5. Tap ⌈Page Down⌉ to move down one slide.

6. Press ⌈Ctrl⌉+⌈End⌉ to move to the last slide.

7. Drag the **scroll box** to the top of the scroll bar to return to slide 1.

PowerPoint Views

You can view a presentation several ways. The views you will use in this chapter are easily accessible in the view bar, which is located at the bottom-right side of the screen.

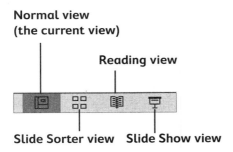

Normal view (the current view)

Reading view

Slide Sorter view   **Slide Show view**

The four views on the view bar include Normal (the view you have been using), Slide Sorter, Reading View, and Slide Show.

- **Normal:** This is the primary view used when creating a presentation. It consists of three areas—the Slides panel on the left side of the screen, the main window in the center of the screen, and the Notes pane at the bottom of the screen, where you can type speaker notes.

- **Slide Sorter:** This view displays all slides in miniature. It's a good way to get a helicopter view of your presentation. In this view you can drag and drop slides with your mouse to rearrange them.

- **Reading View:** With this view, the slide takes over the full PowerPoint screen but not the full Windows screen. The taskbar is still visible at the bottom of the screen, so if you're working with several programs at once, for example, you can switch among programs using the taskbar.

- **Slide Show:** This is the view to use when you're ready to deliver your presentation. All slides take over the full Windows screen.

HANDS-ON 7.4 Explore PowerPoint Views

In this exercise, you will use the view bar to explore other views of a presentation. You will also rearrange slides in Slide Sorter view.

1. Click the **Slide Sorter** button on the view bar.

Your slides now look like thumbnails similar to those in the Slides panel on the left side of the screen in Normal view. Notice the highlighted border around slide 1 that indicates slide 1 is active.

2. Click **slide 2** one time to make it active.

Notice that a highlighted border now surrounds slide 2.

Move Slides in Slide Sorter View

Tip! Slide Sorter view is one of the easiest views to use when you want to rearrange the order of your slides.

3. Follow these steps to move slide 4 to the left of slide 3:

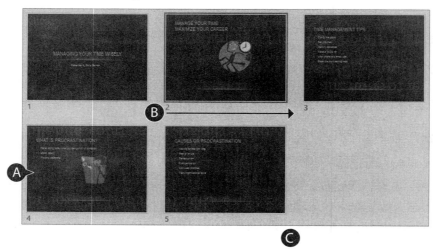

Ⓐ Place the mouse pointer over slide 4 and then press the mouse button.

Ⓑ Drag the slide between slides 2 and 3. The layout of slides on your screen may vary.

Ⓒ Release the mouse button when slide 4 is between slides 2 and 3.

4. Use the same technique to move **slide 5** between slides 3 and 4.

Use Slide Show View

5. Click **slide 1** to make it the active slide.

The active slide is the first slide that will appear when you click the Slide Show button.

6. Click the **Slide Show** button on the view bar.

7. Click the left mouse button to advance to the next slide.

8. Click the left mouse button three more times to move to the last slide.

9. Click the mouse button again and notice the all-black slide.

   How did that get there? PowerPoint put it there for you! It's not a slide that you can see in Normal or Slide Sorter view. This slide gives the presenter an opportunity to wrap up the presentation without the audience looking at PowerPoint's Normal or Slide Sorter view. That would be distracting.

10. Click the mouse button again to return to Slide Sorter view.

    You can see that this view would be distracting for the audience to look at while the presenter is wrapping up.

Use Reading View

11. If necessary, click **slide 1** to make it active.

12. Click the **Reading View** button.

You can see that this view covers the full PowerPoint window but that the Windows taskbar is still visible at the bottom of the screen. If necessary, you can click a program icon on the taskbar to switch to another program while working in PowerPoint.

13. Click the left mouse button anywhere on the slide to advance to the next slide.

14. Continue clicking the left mouse button and notice the black slide at the end of the presentation—just as you saw in Slide Show view.

15. Click through the black slide to return to Slide Sorter view.

16. Click the **Normal** view button on the view bar.

17. Click **Save** 🖫 on the Quick Access toolbar.

18. Choose **File→Close** to close the presentation; leave PowerPoint open.

· ·

Creating a Presentation

Now you will explore the exciting features that allow you to create powerful presentations effortlessly. You'll work with design themes, which add color and interest to your presentation, and with preformatted slide layouts, which make it easy to add text and graphics to your presentation.

As you add clip art to your presentation, you will find that working with clip art in PowerPoint is similar to working with clip art in Word. Once again, you are benefiting from the similarities among programs in a suite.

PowerPoint Themes

PowerPoint's built-in themes present professional-looking color schemes and background graphics that can be applied with the click of a mouse. You can use Live Preview with themes to explore how various themes look before you apply them.

In addition, themes provide a consistent look throughout the presentation in terms of colors, fonts, and other design elements that allow you to concentrate your efforts on your message. Themes can also help set the mood for a presentation with their colors and graphic images.

HANDS-ON 7.5 Use Themes in a Presentation

In this exercise, you will use Live Preview to explore PowerPoint's themes and apply a theme to your presentation.

1. Choose **File→New** and then click the **Blank Presentation** template.

2. Click the **Design** tab on the Ribbon and notice the Themes group.

3. Click the **More** button on the right side of the Themes gallery to display the entire gallery.

4. Hover the mouse pointer over several of the themes and watch as Live Preview displays samples of how a theme would look if you were to apply it to your slide.
   Notice that ToolTips displays the theme name when you hover the mouse pointer over a theme.

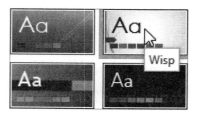

5. If necessary, use ToolTips to locate the Wisp theme.

6. Preview the theme for a moment and then click it to apply it to the slide.

Save the Presentation

7. Choose **File→Save As** and navigate to the **Chapter 07** folder.

8. Type **Efficient Email** in the File Name box at the bottom of the dialog box and then click **Save**.

Typing Text in a Slide

Slides contain dotted boxes called *placeholders*. Placeholders can contain text or objects such as tables, graphs, clip art, and other elements. For now, you will concentrate on adding text to the title and subtitle placeholders in your title slide.

HANDS-ON 7.6 Add Text to a Slide

In this exercise, you will add text to your title slide.

1. Click the **Click to Add Title** text placeholder.
   The placeholder is now selected and its handles (small circles) are visible. You can also see the flashing insertion point, indicating that you can begin to type.

2. Type **Efficient Email** in the text placeholder.
   The appearance of the font is part of the Wisp theme.

3. Click in the **Click to Add Subtitle** placeholder.

4. Type: **Presented by Safia Salman**

5. Save the presentation.
   You are now ready to add a new slide to your presentation.

Slide Layouts

Slide layouts vary based on the text and graphic placeholders embedded in the slide and on the theme selected. The Layout gallery offers different ways to organize your slide contents.

The slide you just completed has the Title Slide layout, which contains title and subtitle placeholders. Next you will use a slide with the Title and Content layout, which contains a title placeholder and a content placeholder.

HANDS-ON 7.7 Add a Slide and Try Different Layouts

In this exercise, you will add a slide and apply different layouts from the Layout gallery.

1. Choose **Home→Slides→New Slide** .

   A new slide is added to the presentation using the default Title and Content layout. Notice the icons that appear in the bottom placeholder. You can click these icons to add elements such as tables, charts, and pictures to the slide.

Change the Slide Layout

The Layout gallery does not use Live Preview, so you have to apply a layout to your slide to see its effect. You'll test some layouts now.

2. Choose **Home→Slides→Layout** .

3. Click **Section Header**.

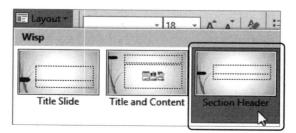

4. Choose **Home→Slides→Layout** .

5. Click the **Two Content** layout.

   Feel free to test other layouts if you wish.

6. Choose **Home→Slides→Layout** 🔳.

7. Apply the **Title and Content** layout.

8. Save the presentation.

Presentation Design Tips

You are now ready to add more content to your presentation. The following are some tried-and-true recommendations from professional presenters. Keeping these guidelines in mind goes a long way in helping you design your presentation like a pro.

Don't Write an Essay

People glaze over when they see dense text. The slide's content should provide a road map of main points for the presenter.

- Use a maximum of eight lines per slide.
- If there's a lot of information, break up the lines over a few slides.
- Don't write in complete sentences; just hit the high points.

Font

It's fun to play with different fonts, but keeping it simple is the recommendation for presentations.

- The font size should be at least 18 points. If possible, go to the back of the room where the presentation will take place and see if you can read the slides.
- Limit the number of fonts to about three per presentation; that includes point size changes.
- Sticking with the fonts the theme provides is a good idea.

Design Theme

Most people recommend a design theme with a dark background, as they are typically more visually appealing, but a dark background can look faded if the room is too light. If possible, check the room conditions first. Also, keep in mind that it's easier on the eyes to read black text on a white (or light) background.

Special Effects

Again, think simple. Special effects like clip art, animations, and slide transitions are fun, but they can detract from your message. Use special effects to emphasize a point—never to entertain.

🖱 HANDS-ON 7.8 Add Content to Your New Slide

In this exercise, you will add text to the title placeholder and the content placeholder.

1. Click the **title placeholder** and type: **Agenda**

2. Click the **bottom placeholder** and type this text:

   `Compose a practical subject line`

   `Write an effective message`

   `Watch your tone`

   `Polish your netiquette`

   `Think before clicking Send`

   `Learn to manage inbox overload`

3. Save the presentation.

Add Pictures and Clip Art

You can insert pictures from your computer or search for clip art and pictures online directly from within PowerPoint. Adding graphic images helps you emphasize key points and add polish to the presentation.

The Insert Pictures search window lets you search for clip art using the Bing search engine and other online resources. Each image is associated with keywords that describe its characteristics. For example, the images shown here can be located by entering the keyword *award*.

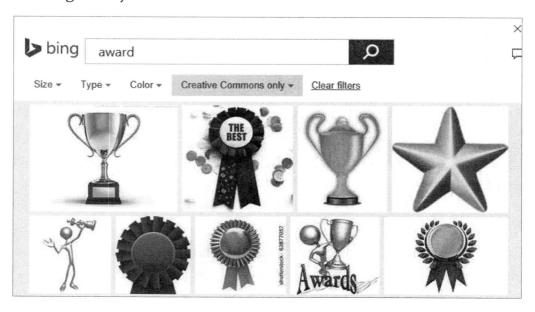

 HANDS-ON 7.9 Add Clip Art to the Presentation

In this exercise, you will add a new slide with a pictures icon embedded in it. You will use the icon to open the Insert Pictures dialog box. Then you will search for a clip art image related to email and insert it in the slide.

1. Choose **Home→Slides→New Slide** 📋 **menu button** ▾.

   This displays the Layout gallery where you can select the layout for the new slide.

2. Choose the **Title and Content** layout.

3. Click the title placeholder and type: `Over 200 Billion Emails Sent Every Day`

4. Click the **Online Pictures** icon in the bottom placeholder.

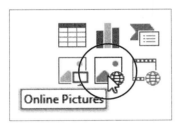

   The Insert Pictures dialog box opens.

5. Follow these steps to search for images:

   Ⓐ Type `email` in the search box.

   Ⓑ Tap ⎡Enter⎤.

6. Follow these steps to insert a clip art image on the slide:

Ⓐ Scroll until you find an image you like. Your results may differ from the figure.

Ⓑ Click an image to select it.

Ⓒ Click **Insert**.

The clip art image is inserted on the slide and replaces the large content placeholder.

Move the Clip Art

7. Hover the mouse pointer over the image. When the mouse pointer changes to a four-headed arrow, drag the image to a position on the screen that you prefer.

Resize the Clip Art

8. Place the mouse pointer over the bottom-right corner handle, and when the pointer changes to a double-headed arrow, drag to resize the image as you deem necessary.

9. Reposition the image, if necessary.

10. Save your presentation.

Delivering the Slide Show

The slides are created and the presentation is complete. The first phase is over. The next phase, delivering the presentation, is just beginning. The successful communication of the slide show depends on the presenter's speaking abilities.

The PowerPoint slide show is secondary to the message the presenter is delivering, and the manner in which you convey the message is critical to grabbing the audience's attention and keeping it. Before you stand in front of an audience, familiarize yourself with the following tips.

Delivery Tips

It's not only *what* you say, it's *how* you say it that makes the difference between an engaging and an unsuccessful presentation. Lead your audience. Help them focus on the message of your presentation. Use the following PEER guidelines to deliver effective presentations:

- **Pace:** Maintain a moderate pace. Speaking too quickly will exhaust your audience and speaking too slowly may put them to sleep. Carry your audience with you as you talk.

- **Emphasis:** Pause for emphasis. As you present, use a brief pause to emphasize your points. Pausing gives your audience time to absorb your message.

- **Eye Contact:** Always face your audience while speaking. A common mistake is to speak while walking or facing the projection screen. Don't waste all of the work you have done in PowerPoint by losing your audience's interest now. If you are speaking from a lectern, resist the temptation to lean on it. Stand tall and look directly at your audience.

- **Relax:** You are enthusiastic and want to convey that tone. However, when you speak, avoid fast movements, pacing, and rushed talking. Your audience will be drawn to your movements and miss the point. Remember that the audience is listening to you to learn; this material may be old hat to you, but it's new to them. Speak clearly, maintain a steady pace, and stay calm.

Navigating in Slide Show View

You use different navigation techniques in a slide show than the ones you used in Normal view. There are several methods you can use to move through a slide show. They include using the mouse, the keyboard, and the Slide Show toolbar.

QUICK REFERENCE: Navigating Slide Shows with the Mouse and Keyboard

Task	Procedure
Advance a slide	Click once with the mouse or tap Spacebar, →, Page Down, or Enter.
Back up a slide	Tap Backspace, Page Up, or ←.
Display the Slide Show toolbar	Move the mouse around on the screen for a moment.

The Slide Show Toolbar

You can use the Slide Show toolbar to navigate during a slide show. It's hidden when a slide show starts but becomes visible in the bottom-left corner when you move your mouse over the screen. If you plan to use the toolbar, it's a good idea to get familiar with it before the presentation; however, you don't need to use it for a simple slide show.

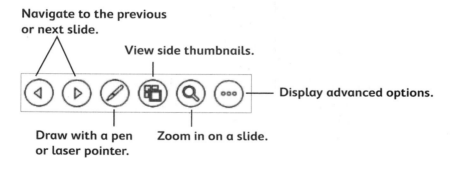

Navigate to the previous or next slide.

View side thumbnails.

Display advanced options.

Draw with a pen or laser pointer.

Zoom in on a slide.

HANDS-ON 7.10 Run the Slide Show

In this exercise, you will use various techniques to navigate in your slide show.

1. Click the **Slide Show** tab on the Ribbon.

2. In the Start Slide Show group, click the **From Beginning** button.

3. Move the mouse pointer on the screen and notice the Slide Show toolbar in the bottom-left corner of the screen.

4. Click the mouse pointer anywhere on the screen to move to the next slide.

5. Tap [Page Down] and then tap [Page Up] twice using the keys near the main keyboard.

   PowerPoint displays the next or previous slide each time you tap these keys.

6. Hover the mouse pointer over the screen to display the Slide Show toolbar and then click **Show All Slides** to display the slide thumbnails.

7. Click the **Agenda** slide.

   As you can see, there are many ways to navigate slides in a slide show.

End the Slide Show

8. Continue to click anywhere on the screen until the last slide appears (the *Over 200 Billion* slide).

9. Click once on the **last slide**.

   The black slide appears.

10. Click anywhere on the **black screen** to exit the slide show and return to the main PowerPoint window.

. . . .

Adding Animations and Transitions

Now that you have completed your slides and run a slide show, you decide to liven up the show using PowerPoint's animation and transition features.

Animating Your Slide Show

Animation brings life to your presentation by affecting how text or objects, such as clip art, enter your slide. The following are a few buttons from the Animation group on the Ribbon to give you an idea of the possibilities available.

If you have lines of text in the Content placeholder, you can have them fade, fly, or float into your slide when you click the mouse button. This keeps your audience focused on the point you are discussing.

⬚ HANDS-ON 7.11 Animate a Slide

In this exercise, you will add life to your slides by applying animations. You will test several different animation options.

1. If necessary, click **slide 2** in the Slides panel to display it.

2. Click anywhere in the bottom placeholder to make it active.

3. Choose **Animations→Animation→Fly In** ✦.

   Wow, pretty interesting! Notice the items are numbered 1 through 6. This is the order in which the items will appear in the slide show when you click the mouse button. Now you will check out how that works in Slide Show view.

4. Click the **Slide Show** 🖵 button on the view bar at the bottom-right corner of the screen.

5. Click the mouse button to see the first point fly into the slide.

6. Click the mouse button to see the second point fly into the slide.

   Can you see how this keeps the audience focused on what the presenter is talking about?

7. Keep clicking the mouse button to see all of the items fly into the slide. The last slide (*Over 200 Billion*) displays.

8. Tap ⎡Esc⎤ to end the slide show.

Try Out More Animations

9. Make sure the second slide is active and then click in the bottom placeholder.

10. Choose **Animations→Animation→More**.

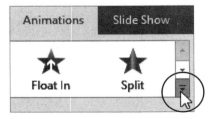

11. Click **Wipe** in the Entrance category to apply and preview that animation.

12. Choose **Animations→Animation→More** and take a few moments to test other animations.

13. When you find an animation you like, apply it to the slide and then try it out in **Slide Show** view.

14. End the slide show and return to **Normal** view.

15. Save your presentation.

Adding Transitions

Transitions are like the effects used by the six o'clock news. When the news commentator finishes one story and transitions to the next, there is typically some type of graphic effect that leads to the next story.

Here are a few buttons located in the Transition to This Slide group on the Ribbon. You can apply a wipe, split, or reveal effect when moving from one slide to another in your presentation.

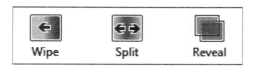

HANDS-ON 7.12 Add Transitions

In this exercise, you will test some transition effects. When you find a transition you like, you will check it out in Slide Show view.

1. If necessary, make **slide 1** the active slide and then choose **Transitions→Transition to This Slide→Split** 🔲.

2. Choose **Transitions→Transition to This Slide→Wipe** 🔲.

3. Take a few moments to test some other transitions.

4. When you find the transition you like, apply it to **slide 1** and then switch to **slide 2** and apply the same transition.

5. Switch to **slide 3** and apply the same transition.
   Although you could apply a different transition to each slide, it would likely be distracting for the audience. Some of PowerPoint's transitions are pretty lively and possibly distracting. Think "subtle" when selecting a transition.

6. Make **slide 1** active and then watch your presentation in **Slide Show** view.

7. Save and close the presentation.

Self-Assessment

Check your knowledge of this chapter's key concepts and skills by completing the Self-Assessment.

Page number

1. You can use Live Preview to explore how themes look before applying them.   **true false** _____

2. Themes provide a consistent look throughout a presentation in terms of colors, fonts, and other design elements.   **true false** _____

3. The Slide Show toolbar provides the only methods for navigating in a slide show.   **true false** _____

4. You can add only clip art pictures that you already have on your hard drive.   **true false** _____

5. Animation affects how text or objects enter your slide.   **true false** _____

6. You use Slide Sorter view when you're ready to deliver a presentation.   **true false** _____

7. Which view displays the presentation in the full Windows screen?

    A. Normal

    B. Slide Show

    C. Reading View

    D. Slide Sorter

    Page number: _____

8. Which of these is NOT a method of navigating through a presentation in Normal view?

    A. Dragging the scroll box

    B. Using the Slide Show toolbar

    C. Using the Slides panel

    D. Using the Next Slide and Previous Slide buttons on the scroll bar

    Page number: _____

9. Which of these is NOT a slide layout?

    A. Title and Content

    B. Title Slide

    C. Blank

    D. Clip Art

    Page number: _____

10. Which of these is NOT available on the view bar?

    A. Print Preview

    B. Slide Sorter

    C. Normal

    D. Slide Show

    Page number: _____

Skill Builders

....

SKILL BUILDER 7.1 Present the Giraffes

Your niece Hayden heard about your giraffe graph and is intrigued! She has asked you to come to her school to give a presentation on giraffes. In this exercise, you will use the picture icon embedded in a slide to insert a photograph of the giraffes. Then you will copy your giraffe graph into the presentation.

1. Choose **File**→**New** and click the **Blank Presentation** template.

Apply a Theme

2. Click the **Design** tab.

3. Click the **More** button on the right side of the Themes gallery to display the entire gallery.

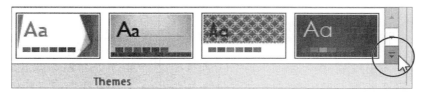

4. Use ToolTips to locate the Organic theme and apply it to the slide.

5. Click the **title placeholder** and type: `My Trip to the Zoo`

6. Click the **subtitle placeholder** and type: `By Piper Goodspeed`

Add a New Slide and Insert a Photograph

7. Choose **Home**→**Slides**→**New Slide** .

8. Click in the **title placeholder** and type: `The Giraffes`

9. Click the **Pictures** icon.

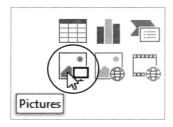

10. Navigate to your **Chapter 07** folder and double-click **sb-Giraffe Picture**.

Add a New Slide and Change the Layout

11. Choose **Home→Slides→New Slide** .

12. Choose **Home→Slides→Layout**.

13. Choose the **Title Only** layout.

14. Click the **title placeholder** and type: `Graph of Giraffe Heights`

15. Save the presentation as: `sb-My Trip to the Zoo`

Next you will copy a graph from an Excel file. You haven't switched between software programs before, so saving at this point is just an extra precaution against losing data.

Start Excel and Copy a Graph into the Slide

16. Start Excel.

17. Click the **Open Other Workbooks** link at the bottom of the left pane.

18. Double-click **This PC** in the middle column.

19. Navigate to your **Chapter 07** folder and double-click **sb-Giraffe Graph**.

20. If a yellow bar appears across the top of the Excel window indicating a Security Warning or that the spreadsheet was opened in Protected View, click **Enable Content** or **Enable Editing** (whichever displays) to allow you to copy the chart.

21. If a message appears indicating that some links in the workbook cannot be updated, click **Continue** or **Don't Update** (whichever displays).

22. If necessary, click the **outside border** of the graph to select it.

23. Choose **Home→Clipboard→Copy**.

24. Click the **PowerPoint** icon on the Windows taskbar to switch to PowerPoint.

25. Choose **Home→Clipboard→Paste**.

The graph appears in the slide; notice that it has taken on the colors of the Organic theme.

The graph is a little too big, so you'll resize the graph next.

Resize and Move the Graph

26. Position the mouse pointer in the upper-left corner of the graph frame and notice that the pointer changes to a double-headed arrow.

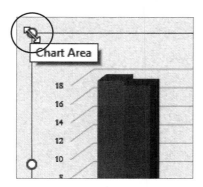

27. Press the mouse button and drag down and to the right until the graph is below the title.

The graph is not perfectly centered vertically on the slide.

28. Position the mouse pointer on the bottom-center handle of the graph frame and the pointer changes to a double-headed arrow.

29. Press the mouse button and drag up until the graph fits in the white area of the slide without overlapping the border.

30. Position the mouse pointer on the border of the graph frame so the pointer changes to a four-headed arrow.

31. Press the mouse button and drag a little to the left until the graph is well centered on the slide; release the mouse button.

32. Make **slide 1** active; review your presentation in Slide Show view.

33. Save and close the presentation.

34. Click the **Excel** icon on the taskbar to restore the Excel window.

35. Click the **X** in the top-right corner of the Excel window to close it.

SKILL BUILDER 7.2 Add Animation and Transitions to a Presentation

In this exercise, you will open a presentation and add some pizzazz using animation and transitions.

1. Open **sb-Tropical Getaways** from your **Chapter 07** folder.

2. Click the **slide 2** thumbnail icon in the Slides panel on the left side of the screen.
   Notice that slide 2 contains bullet points. That's part of the design for the Facet theme used in this presentation.

Add Animation to a Slide

3. Click in the bottom-left placeholder to select it.
   You should now see a dotted-line box surrounding the placeholder.

4. Choose **Animations→Animation→Fade ★**.
   Notice during the preview that each item fades in separately, one after the other.

5. Switch to **Slide Show 🖵** view and click the mouse button four times to display each of the first four destinations.
   Hmmm, that seems a little tedious. It might be better if the four destinations appeared at the same time.

6. Right-click a blank area of the slide and choose **End Show**.

Tip! If you select (highlight) all four of the items and then apply the animation, they will behave as one unit.

7. Place the **I-beam ⌶** mouse pointer to the left of the *T* in *Tahiti* and drag down to select all four destinations.

8. Choose **Animations→Animation→Fade ★**.
   Notice during the preview that all four items fade in together as one unit.

9. Switch to **Slide Show 🖵** view; click the mouse button once and all four items display at the same time.

10. End the slide show.

11. Drag to select all four items in the bottom-right placeholder and apply the **Fade** animation.

Apply Animation to Additional Slides

12. Switch to **slide 3**.

13. Click in the **bottom-left placeholder** to select it.

14. Choose **Animations→Animation→Fly In** ✷.

    Notice that during the preview all four items fly in together. How did that happen when you didn't select all four items first? It's because the last three items are sub-bullets (indented) below the main bullet. That causes PowerPoint to assume that the items should act as one unit. (You create sub-bullets in a placeholder by tapping the Tab *key.)*

15. Click in the **bottom-right placeholder** to select it and apply the **Fly In** animation.

16. Go to **slide 4**, click the **bottom placeholder**, and apply the **Float In** animation. (You may have to use the More button in the Animation group to locate Float In.)

    This time PowerPoint assumes that each of the main bullets and their associated sub-bullets are a unit. You have two main bullets, so each one floats in with its associated sub-bullets.

17. Go to **slide 5** and apply the animation of your choice to the bulleted text.

18. Press Ctrl + Home to return to the beginning of the presentation.

19. Switch to **Slide Show** view and enjoy the show.

    Remember, it's fun to play with different animations, but you don't want to distract the audience. For actual business-related presentations, consider using only one or two animation styles for the entire show.

Add Transitions to the Slide Show

Using a variety of transitions could be distracting, so you will apply the same transition to all slides. Using Slide Sorter view is an easy way to apply the same transition to all slides at the same time.

20. Click the **Slide Sorter** ⊞ view on the view bar.

21. If necessary, click **slide 1** to make it active.

    It will have a highlighted border around it if it's active.

Tip! If you select a slide and then hold down the Shift key and click another slide, PowerPoint also selects all the slides in between.

22. Press Shift and click **slide 6**; release the Shift key.

    All six slides now have a highlighted border, meaning all six slides are selected.

23. Choose **Transitions→Transition to This Slide→Push** ▣.

View Your Final Presentation

24. Click **slide 1** to reselect slide 1 and deselect the other slides.

25. Switch to **Slide Show** view and run the slide show.

26. Save and close the presentation.

27. Exit PowerPoint.

Introducing Databases

In this chapter, you will be introduced to database concepts and work with Access tables, the starting point of all databases. Have you ever wondered how sportscasters come up with fun and interesting facts about teams and players in a flash? Have you been taken by surprise when a customer service agent suddenly begins to recite your name, address, and a detailed purchase history? In most cases, these people have access to a powerful database from which they obtain the information.

LEARNING OBJECTIVES

- Identify database objects and the functions they perform
- Identify table features
- Create database tables
- Identify and choose data types
- Print a datasheet

📂 Project: Creating a Database

Winchester Web Design is a small website development company. The company specializes in building websites for small businesses. You have been asked to build a database to help the company manage its employee, customer, and sales data. You'll get started by exploring objects in an existing database. Then you'll create a database and work with tables.

What Is Access?

It is likely that you routinely interact with databases. If you make an online purchase, your order information goes into a database. The database might be used to track your order status, product likes and reviews, past orders, or future promotions. If you post or like something on your Facebook account, that information is maintained in a database. If you search for or store a telephone number, that information is likely kept in a database. It is quite possible you have been using databases without even knowing it! Here, you will be introduced to what a database is and gain a better understanding of related terms, explore a sample database, and finally, create your own!

While there are many definitions of a database, you can think of a database as an organized collection of related data files or tables. For example, a company might organize its information by both customers (external to the business) and employees (internal to the business). While the data relate to the same business, the types of data provided for customers and employees will likely differ.

Databases are the epicenter of our digital world.

Types of Databases

Large organizations typically use large custom-designed databases specifically for that company or industry. When you make travel plans, you are using a database that is specific to the airline industry. It contains real-time data, meaning that if there is only one seat left on a plane, whoever selects and pays for the seat first gets the reservation. If you are a small business owner, you may use a database like Microsoft Access to track information about your customers, products, and employees. Access provides the tools needed to let small organizations create, use, and maintain databases.

Open and Save an Access Database

Each time you start Access, the Backstage view displays options for opening an existing file, creating a new blank database, or selecting from a number of pre-built templates. If you're creating a new database, Access will immediately prompt you to save the file in your desired storage location. You must save your file first because the database needs to constantly make updates to data as it is entered or edited.

HANDS-ON 8.1 Start Access and Open a Database

In this exercise, you will start the Access program and open an existing database.

1. If necessary, start your computer.

2. Click the **Start** ⊞ button in the bottom-left corner of the screen.

3. Scroll down the alphabetical list and click **Access 2016**.
   The Access program loads and Backstage view is displayed. Recently used databases appear on the left, and you can create new databases from the list of templates.

4. **Maximize** ▫ the Access window if it isn't already maximized.

5. Choose **Open Other Files** near the lower-left side of the window.

6. Click the **Browse** button, navigate to your **Chapter 08** folder, and open the **Win Web Design** database file.

7. Click **Enable Content** if the Security Warning bar displays.
   The Security Warning appears whenever a database file is opened for the first time. You should never open files unless you know and trust the file sender. The database objects are shown in the Navigation pane on the left.

8. Keep Access open, as you will continue to use the database to explore the Access environment.

Database Objects and the Access Window

The Access window includes the Ribbon, Navigation pane, and work area. A database object is a structure used to store, retrieve, or display data. The four Access objects are tables, queries, forms, and reports. The database objects are displayed in the Navigation pane on the left side of the window. The work area is where you create, modify, or work with database objects.

DATABASE OBJECT TYPES

Access Object	What It Does
Table	Tables contain the database's data, and they let you enter, edit, delete, or view records in a row and column layout that is similar to that used in an Excel worksheet. A record contains information about an individual person, place, or item.
Form	Forms are used to view, edit, and add data one table record at a time.
Query	Queries are used to search for specific table records using criteria and to sort and perform calculations on the results.
Report	Reports are printable database objects that can display, group, and summarize data from tables and/or queries.

HANDS-ON 8.2 Use Database Objects and Enter and Edit Data

In this exercise, you will open and view the four Access object types.

1. Take a moment to explore the Access window noticing the various tables, queries, forms, and reports in the Navigation pane.

Explore a Table

2. Double-click the **Customers** table in the Objects list of the Navigation pane to open it in the work area within Datasheet View.

   Notice that the table, which is in Datasheet View, looks like a worksheet with columns and rows. Datasheet View lets you view, add, and edit table records. One benefit of Datasheet View is it lets you see more than one record at a time.

3. Click in the **first empty Cust ID** cell at the bottom of the CustID column.

4. Type **AdamsA** and tap ⌷Tab⌷ to complete the entry and move the insertion point to the next field.

   Notice the pencil icon highlighted in yellow. This indicates the current record is active and being created or edited.

	⊞	ThibeauxP	Thibeaux	Pierre
	⊞	WinklerS	Winkler	Samuel
✎	⊞	AdamsA		
✳				

   Cust ID is known as a primary key field in this table, so each Cust ID must be unique.

5. Type **Adams** in the Last Name field and tap ⌷Tab⌷.

6. Enter **Anthony** as the First Name, **23 Pine St** as the street address, and **Bradenton** as the city.

7. Click the **drop-down menu** button ▼ in the ST field and choose **FL** from the list of states.

   ST is an example of a field with properties that make data entry easy and accurate.

8. Complete the record as follows, making sure you tap ⌷Tab⌷ after entering the information in each cell.

   Tapping ⌷Tab⌷ after entering a full row of data completes the record, saving it in the database. As you enter the telephone number, just type the digits; Access will automatically format the entry for you.

   - ZIP: **34210**

   - Telephone: **(941) 555-3648**

   - Email: **AAdams@email.com**

   - Notes: **Call for delivery.**

9. Choose **Home→Views→View menu button** ▼ and then choose **Design View** ☒.

   Fields contain pieces of data in records such as zip codes, telephone numbers, email addresses, or notes. Each object type can be created or edited using Design View. Tables Design View is where fields can be added, removed, or edited and field properties can be set.

10. Click the **View menu** button ▼ and choose **Datasheet View** ▦.

    Notice the Anthony Adams record is now the second record in the table. It moved up because the records are sorted in ascending order using the Cust ID field.

Explore a Form

Now you will explore a form that is based on the Customers table. Forms help facilitate effective data entry by displaying one record at a time.

11. Double-click **Customers Form** in the Forms section of the Navigation pane.

Notice the form displays all fields from the Customers table but only one record is visible.

12. Locate the Record bar at the bottom of the form.

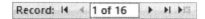

13. Click the **Next Record** ▶ button to view the Anthony Adams record you just entered.

14. Click in the **Notes** box and type `after 10:00` at the end of the note (that is, "Call for Delivery after 10:00").

15. Click the **Next Record** ▶ button again to complete the edit.

This edit has now been saved in the Customers table.

Explore a Query

Now you will explore a query that is based on the Customers table. Queries choose specific database records using criteria that you specify.

16. Double-click **Customers Query** in the Queries section of the Navigation pane.

The query results look like a table displayed in Datasheet View, but the query only displays some of the fields from the underlying Customers table and records where the City is equal to Bradenton.

17. Click the **View menu** button ▼ on the Ribbon and choose **Design View** ☑.

The query has fields from the Customers table and the criterion (a single criteria) bradenton. *This is an example of a simple query based on a single table. Queries can draw data from multiple tables and can include more sophisticated criteria.*

18. Choose **Design→Results→Run** ! to run the query and display only the Bradenton results.

Explore a Report

Now you will explore a report that uses multiple tables, including the Customers table.

19. Double-click **Invoice Details Report** in the Reports section.

Take a moment to scroll through and observe the report.

20. Click the **View menu** button ▼ on the Ribbon and choose **Design View** ⊾.

The Report design grid may look complicated, but it's easy to create a robust report using the Access Report Wizard. The design grid can then be used to make modifications once the foundation has been set with the Wizard.

21. Click the **View menu** button ▼ on the Ribbon and choose **Report View** 🖻, which is great for viewing reports.

22. Follow these steps to explore the object tabs and to close an object:

Ⓐ Switch between open objects using the tabs.

Ⓑ Click the **Close Object** button to close the objects one at a time.

23. Choose **File→Close** to close the database.

The data you entered and edited is automatically saved by the database.

Introducing Tables

A table is the starting point for entering, finding, and reporting useful information located in your database. A database can have separate tables, each tracking different types of data. A business might use a table to keep track of customer billing or employee contact information.

Table Features

Data are meaningful units of information such as names, numbers, dates, and descriptions organized for reference or analysis. The data stored in the Winchester Web Design Group database might include customer first and last names, business names, telephone numbers, and other important information.

A field is the smallest meaningful unit of information about a person, place, or item. Individually, each field represents a piece of data. Together the fields provide information. In most databases, fields are displayed in columns.

A record is a collection of related fields about a person, place, or item, such as a single customer or employee. A collection of related records makes up a table. In most databases, records are displayed in rows.

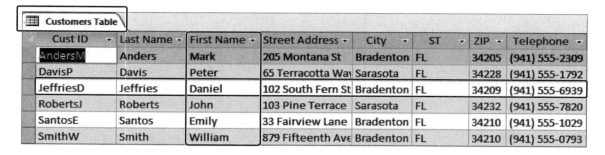

First Name field and JeffriesD record in Customers table

Field Data Types

If you have ever filled out an online form, you might have seen instant formatting of some fields. When typing in currency values, the dollar sign and decimal point may appear automatically, and when entering a date, the slashes between month, day, and year spontaneously appear. This can be accomplished by assigning a data type to the field. A data type sets the characteristics of a particular field, identifying the type of values it may hold, such as alphanumeric text, or numbers, or dates, yes/no values, or even a hyperlink.

Primary Key Fields

Almost every database table should have a primary key field. A primary key is a unique identifier for each record in the table. Examples of fields that would make good primary keys are Social Security numbers, student IDs, or email addresses. Using a student ID as a primary key ensures that each student is uniquely identified in a student database table. Two students may have identical names, but they will never have identical student ID numbers.

Creating a Table in a New Database

Instead of using a database that someone else has prepared, you can design your own using a blank database template in Access. Tables are the starting point for databases and this shows up when a new blank database is first created. The new table has a single primary key field as a starting point for the database.

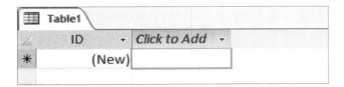

The starting point in a blank database

HANDS-ON 8.3 Create a Blank Database and Add a Table

In this exercise, you will create a new blank database and add an Invoices table in Datasheet View.

1. If necessary, start Access and choose **Blank Desktop Database**.

2. Click **Browse Folders** 📁 and save the database in your **Chapter 08** folder as:
   Datasheet
   Access is the only Office application that requires you to save a new file (the database) before you can begin working.

3. Click the **Create** button, and a new table will appear.

4. Follow these steps to change the name of the ID field and set the data type for a second field:

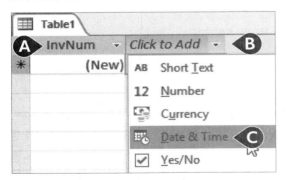

Ⓐ Double-click the **ID** field name and type **InvNum** as the new name. This will be the primary key field.

Ⓑ Tap [Tab] to go to the second column and, if necessary, choose **Click to Add** to display the data type list.

Ⓒ Choose **Date & Time**.
   Once the data type is selected, the heading for the new field becomes Field1.

5. Replace *Field1* with the name **InvDate** and tap [Tab] to move to a new field.
   Your table currently has a primary key field and one Date/Time field.

6. Choose **Short Text** as the data type for the third field and change the field name to: **EmpID**

7. Tap Tab, choose **Short Text** for the fourth field data type, and change the field name to: **CustID**

   Your simple table with four fields is now set up and ready for data to be entered.

8. Click in the **empty InvDate** field (you might have to click twice) and type **12/15/2016**.

9. Tap Tab and type **JFW** as the EmpID.

10. Tap Tab, type **SmithW** as the CustID and then tap Tab again to begin a new record.

11. Enter the data for these three additional records:

    The InvNum primary key field is automatically numbered because it has an AutoNumber property set.

InvNum	InvDate	EmpID	CustID
1	12/15/2016	JFW	SmithW
2	12/2/2016	MJW	SantosE
3	1/1/2016	JMM	SantosE
4	11/30/2016	JMM	SmithW

12. Choose **File→Save** or click the **Save** button on the Quick Access toolbar and save the table as: **Invoices**

    You will print the table in the next exercise.

Printing Data and Closing a Database

Previewing and printing table datasheets and other Access objects, such as reports, is easily done using the File→Print command. Sometimes paper printouts are necessary, and you may also find they are an effective way to check a database for accuracy. When you close a database using the File→Close command, Access will prompt you to save changes to any unsaved open objects, such as tables, forms, reports, and queries.

HANDS-ON 8.4 Print a Datasheet and Close the Database

In this exercise, you will preview and print a database table and then close it.

1. Make sure the **Datasheet** database is open and the Invoices table is displayed in Datasheet View.

   Tables are displayed in Datasheet View by double-clicking them in the Navigation pane on the left side of the Access window.

2. Choose **File**→**Print** and then choose **Print Preview**.

3. Notice the preview of how the datasheet will look when printed and then take a moment to explore the Print Preview toolbar options.

4. Choose **Print Preview**→**Print** and then click **OK** if you want to actually print the datasheet; otherwise, choose **Print Preview**→**Close Print Preview**.

5. Choose **File**→**Close** to close the database, choosing **Yes** if you are prompted to save changes to your table.

Self-Assessment

Check your knowledge of this chapter's key concepts and skills by completing the Self-Assessment.

Page number

1. Zara should use a form if she wants to display one record at a time on her screen.　　**true　false**　_____

2. A primary key uniquely identifies each record in a table.　　**true　false**　_____

3. Which database object is used for storing data?

   A. Form

   B. Query

   C. Report

   D. Table

   Page number: _____

4. Short text, hyperlink, and numeric are examples of?

   A. Primary keys

   B. Records

   C. Queries

   D. Data types

   Page number: _____

5. Which table feature is shown within the rectangle?

InvNum ⌄	Invoice Date ⌄	Emp ID ⌄	Cust ID ⌄
1	3/15/2012	JFW	SmithW
2	4/2/2012	MJW	SantosE
3	5/11/2012	JMM	SantosE
4	5/30/2012	JMM	SmithW

   ⊞ Invoices

   A. Field

   B. Record

   C. Relationship

   D. Primary key

   Page number: _____

6. Which database object should be used to locate all customers who live in Springfield, Illinois, and to then sort the results in order by zip code?

   A. Form

   B. Query

   C. Report

   D. Table

   Page number: _____

7. Which database object is best for viewing and editing one record at a time?

   A. Table

   B. Form

   C. Query

   D. Report

   Page number: _____

8. The names, addresses, and phone numbers for 5,000 customers are stored in a database as which of the following?

   A. 5,000 fields

   B. 5,000 records

   C. 5,000 tables

   D. A single object

   Page number: _____

Skill Builders

Enter and Edit Database Records

First Perk is a coffee shop that tracks sales using an Access database. In this exercise, you will update pricing and add several new items.

1. Start Access and choose **Open Other Files**. (Or, if Access is already open, choose **File→Open**.)

2. Click the **Browse** button, navigate to your **Chapter 08** folder, and double-click the **First Perk** database file.

3. Open the **Items** table in Datasheet View by double-clicking it in the Navigation pane.

4. Click in the **Price** field for the Coffee item and change the price from 1.50 to **2.00**.

   Note that dollar signs $ are automatically displayed in the Price field because the field is formatted with a Currency number format.

5. Change the price of Coffee-Decaf to **2.00** and change the price of Espresso Shot to **2.50**.

6. Now add the following items to the database:

ItemName	Price
Latte	3.25
Cappuccino	3.25
Mocha	3.50
Green Tea	2.50
Earl Grey	2.50

   Note that Access automatically numbers the ItemNumber field for you because it is set up as an AutoNumber field type.

7. Feel free to print a copy of the datasheet.

8. Close the table and then choose **File→Close** to close the database.

SKILL BUILDER 8.2 Create a Table in Datasheet View

In this exercise, you will create a new database and a table using Datasheet View.

1. Start Access. Or, if Access is already open, choose **File**.

2. Choose **Blank Desktop Database** and then click the **Browse Folders** 🖿 button and save the database in your **Chapter 08** folder as K4C.

3. Click the **Create** button to start a new database.

4. Double-click the **ID** heading and change the text to StID.

   This will be the primary key field with autonumbering, so your records will automatically get numbered.

5. Tap ⌷Tab⌷, choose **Short Text** as the data type, and change the heading from *Field1* to StLName.

6. Add StFName, StAdd, StCity, StST, StZIP, StPhone, and StAvail as fields with the Short Text data type.

7. Choose **File→Save** or click the **Save** 🖫 button on the Quick Access toolbar and save your table as Staff.

8. Click the first empty cell in the **StLName** field and enter the following records using these guidelines:

   - Tap the ⌷Tab⌷ key to complete your entries.

   - Enter hyphens in the phone field, as the field is not set up to automatically enter them for you.

   - Widen the columns as necessary by double-clicking the right borders of the column headings you want to widen.

   - Strive for 100% accuracy when entering data, which requires including spaces between characters when called for and verifying the capitalization of upper- and lowercase letters.

⊞ Staff								
StID ▾	StLName ▾	StFName ▾	StAdd ▾	StCity ▾	StST ▾	StZIP ▾	StPhone ▾	StAvail ▾
1	Bryant	Matthew	12 Macintosh St	Sarasota	FL	34022	941-555-7523	Thursday
2	Earle	Kevin	77 Kingfisher Ct	Sarasota	FL	34024	941-555-1368	Monday

9. Close the Staff table, saving the changes, and then choose **File→Close** to close the database.

10. Exit Access.

Glossary

AutoComplete   Feature that recognizes certain kinds of entries, such as dates, and offers to complete them for you as you type

AutoCorrect   Feature that automatically corrects commonly misspelled words as you type, based on a built-in dictionary

Backstage view   Feature that contains commands to manage your files, such as Open, Save, and Print; available from the File tab

cell   Small rectangle that appears wherever a column and row intersect in a table or spreadsheet

character formatting   How text or numerical characters look; includes font type, font style, font size, font color, and special effects

clip art   Photos and images you can use in your documents

Clipboard   Area in your computer's memory where data that you cut or copy is temporarily stored before pasting it in another location

Compatibility Mode   Documents created in some earlier versions of Microsoft Office open in Compatibility Mode; this limits the application to using only features available in earlier versions

contextual tabs   Tabs on the Ribbon that appear only when certain objects are selected; for example, the Table Tools®Layout contextual tab appears only when a table is selected in Word or PowerPoint

Crop   Feature used to hide any unwanted portions of a graphic image

data   Information such as names, numbers, dates, descriptions, etc., organized for reference or analysis

databases   Collections of related information (e.g., name and address list); typically stored in an electronic format that allows users to select and sort records of information

Datasheet View   Displays actual data values

Design View   Where form, query, and report layout is defined; shows field names and labels, as well as other objects that can be displayed

field   Column of information in a database

file   Collection of data saved on your hard drive or other storage media; saved documents are called files

file format   Consistent pattern for storing information in a computer file; application programs normally have a special file format that they use by default; examples are *.docx* (Word), *.xlsx* (Excel), *.pptx* (PowerPoint), and *.accdb* (Access)

Find and Replace   Feature that finds a word, phrase, or format that you specify and, optionally, replaces it with another word, phrase, or format

folder   Area in a computer filing system in which you store files (documents); can be made on storage devices, such as USB drives, hard drives, or network drives

forms   Database screens used to enter, edit, and view data for an individual record in a layout that is more convenient and attractive than a table datasheet layout

formula   Equation that performs calculations on values in a spreadsheet

Formula Bar   Data in the active cell appears in the Formula Bar

Freeze Panes   Excel feature that allows you to freeze column or row headings so they remain visible on the screen when you scroll through a spreadsheet

function   Formula built into Excel that performs calculations on cells in a table or spreadsheet

handles   Small squares or circles that surround an object when it is selected; you can drag a handle with the mouse pointer to resize an object

I-beam   Shape of the mouse pointer when in the typing area of a document; resembles a capital "I"

icon   Small GUI (graphical user interface) that represents an object, such as a folder in which you store your files

insertion point   Blinking indicator where text will appear on the screen; when typing you must position the insertion point at the desired location before typing; also referred to as the cursor

Live Preview   When pointing at formatting commands on the Ribbon, Live Preview displays how the format would appear on selected text and objects without actually applying the format

mathematical operators   Signs used for addition, subtraction, multiplication, and division

Mini toolbar   Contains frequently used formatting commands; appears when you select cells or text or when you right-click on cells or text

Name box   Displays the address of the active cell

Navigation pane   In Word, used to find text in a document; enter a search term and all instances of the term appear in the Results list, which you can use to navigate to the term. In Access, an objects panel that lists existing database objects (specifically tables, queries, forms, and reports)

nonprinting characters   Symbols that represent typing elements, such as spaces and tabs; you can display the symbols on the screen, but they will not appear on the printed page

object   A database structure used to store or reference data

presentation program   Software application (such as PowerPoint) that allows you to create dynamic multimedia presentations that can be displayed on your computer or projected on a screen

primary key   Unique identifier in a database field (e.g., a Social Security number); helps ensure that a database does not contain duplicate records

queries   Objects used to select, search, sort, and extract table data based on criteria and conditions; display results in a row-and-column format

Quick Access toolbar   Toolbar that contains buttons for frequently used commands; can be customized by adding command buttons

range   Group of adjacent cells in a spreadsheet, such as A1:A100

real-time data   Data that is updated and shown at the speed at which a computer receives and processes information

record   Row of information in a database

Redo   Feature that allows you to successively repeat your last action(s), starting with the most recent

relative reference   Excel automatically changes cell addresses in copied formulas and functions relative to where they are copied

reports   Database pages that present processed and summarized data from tables and queries as mean-ingful information in an easy-to-read format; designed to be printed

Ribbon   Band running across the top of the screen that contains software commands for Office 2016 applications; organized in tabs that relate to a particular type of activity and groups that contain related commands

scroll bar   Means of moving to different areas of a document

select   To choose an object or to highlight text in order to manipulate it in some way

selection bar   In Word, the white space at the left margin from which you can select text

Slide Layout   Preset layout of placeholder boxes on a PowerPoint slide

Slide Show   View used in PowerPoint when delivering a presentation

Sort   Arranges data in alphabetic, numeric, or date order

Spelling & Grammar checker   Feature that monitors your spelling and grammar as you type; underlines suspected misspellings/grammar errors with squiggly red/blue lines. Right-clicking displays a pop-up menu of possible corrections.

spreadsheet   Document that allow you to organize data in columns and rows, analyze data, and perform calculations on data; also known as worksheet

suite   Collection of software applications sold as one package; less expensive than buying the individual applications; applications typically contain features that work in a similar fashion

tables   In Access, files or collections of related records; contain the data used in all other database objects

task pane   Screen element that contains links and icons you click to issue commands to the computer

template   Serves as a pattern for new documents, which take on the template's characteristics, such as font choice, line spacing, margin settings, boilerplate text, etc.

theme   Set of formatting selections you can apply to a document; includes colors, graphic elements, and fonts all designed to work well together

toolbar   GUI (graphical user interface) containing buttons that represent commands

ToolTips   Small pop-up notes that appear when you hover the mouse pointer over a Ribbon or toolbar command; contain a description of the command

typing area   In Word, the area between the margins of a page; where you type

Undo   Feature that successively undoes changes you make in a document, starting with the last one

USB flash drive   Stores your data on a flash memory chip; plug it into a USB port on any computer and Windows recognizes it as an additional disk drive

views   Varying ways you can look at a document, spreadsheet, or presentation; optimized for specific types of work

word processor   Software application that allows you to electronically create and edit text

Word Wrap   Feature that wraps to the next line a long string of text that extends beyond the right margin

work area   Main part of the screen where you design tables, queries, forms, and reports; where you enter data into tables and forms

worksheet   *See* spreadsheet

WordArt   Graphic image of stylized, decorative text

Index